# "THE BOY LOOKED AT JOHNNY.

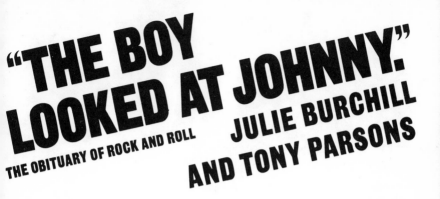

# "THE BOY LOOKED AT JOHNNY."

## THE OBITUARY OF ROCK AND ROLL

### JULIE BURCHILL AND TONY PARSONS

PLUTO PRESS

First published 1978 by Pluto Press Limited,
Unit 10 Spencer Court, 7 Chalcot Road, London NW1 8LH

ISBN 0 86104 030 9

Designed by Terry Seago
Cover photograph: *Johnny Rotten:* Syndication International Ltd

Typeset by Moorgate Typesetting Co Ltd, London
Printed in Great Britain by Cox & Wyman Ltd,
London, Fakenham and Reading

Picture acknowledgements: The *New York Dolls:* Claude Vanheye,
London Features International Ltd; *Iggy Pop and David Bowie:*
Chalkie Davies; *Scabies, Lemmy and Gaye Advert:* Paul Slattery;
*Debbie Blondie:* Pennie Smith; *Joan Jett:* Chalkie Davies; *Tom
Robinson:* Paul Cox, London Features International Ltd; *Poly
Styrene:* Gus Stewart; *Johnny Thunders:* Gus Stewart; *Julie Burchill
and Tony Parsons* (back cover): Pennie Smith.

**DEDICATIONS**

With love to Pennie Smith, Danny Baker and John May
To Joan Jett and Poly Styrene
To Allan V. Harrison and Pete Mannheim
To Menachim Begin
To Charles Shaar Murray, Angus McKinnon, Denis O'Regan, the
Tom Robinson Band and everyone else on the same side at
Lewisham, 1977
And especially for our parents

The authors, Spring 1978, Carnaby Street, London W.1


Dedications are traditionally left entirely to authors but in this case
the publishers feel it important to dissociate themselves from line
four on this page.

"YOU KNOW WE WENT FOR A RIDE
AND THEN THERE WAS BILL
—AND JERRY—AND ARTHUR WA

"WE WON'T BE BACK FOR A WHILE.
AND JOHNNY—AND DAVIE
A KID THAT I ONCE KNEW..."
NEW YORK DOLLS

# "GEE, SUCCESS HAS SWOLLEN MY HEAD."

### DEBBIE BLONDIE

# "ONE LITTLE PIGGY WENT TO MARKET, ONE LITTLE PIGGY PLAYED KEYBOARDS."

IGGY POP AND DAVID BOWIE

"WE CAME UP FROM NOWHERE
AND WE'RE GOING
STRAIGHT BACK THERE."
SCABIES, LEMMY AND GAYE ADVERT

"IT TURNS MY STOMACH."
JOAN JETT

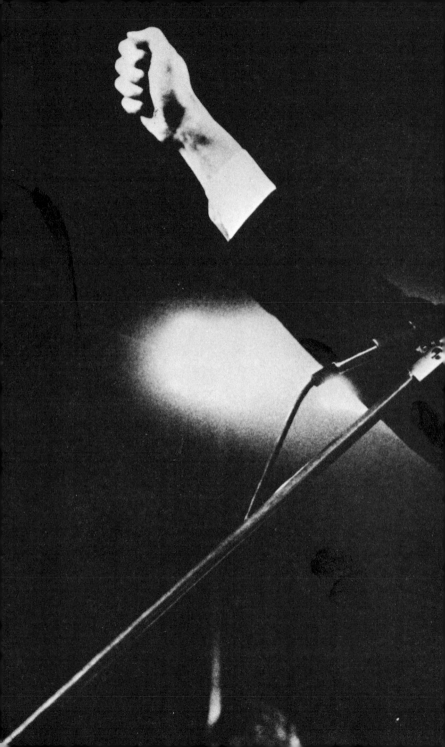

"YOU, YOU WILL BE KING."
TOM ROBINSON

# "AND YOU, YOU WILL BE QUEEN."
**POLY STYRENE**

"I COULDA BEEN A CONTENDER..."

JOHNNY THUNDERS

# GERMS

Bob Dylan broke his neck – close, but no cigar.

Sealed integrity is reserved for the feted self-immolated. Choking on their own idolised vomit allowed a fistful of White Youth Culture luminaries – Brian Jones, Jimi Hendrix, Janis Joplin, Jim Morrison – to escape the fate of life-sucking godhead, as did their Fifties antecedents.

Fast-living, young-dying, good-looking icons like Eddie Cochran (killed in a car crash), Gene Vincent (fatally shell-shocked from Cochran's last ride), Buddy Holly, Richie Valens, Big Bopper (victims of the same plane crash), Jerry Lee Lewis, Chuck Berry (two primal paedophiles), Elvis Presley (drafted down the middle of the road), Little Richard (who – God forgive him – got religion) – all killed or castrated before their decade was dead.

But the Sixties was a decade of iron-lung dinosaurs washing their hands of the blood of teen idealism – sated, sanitised and bloated after gorging on the carnal/chemical/mass-worship fruit of their assault on the heights.

Artistic pretension became self-parody as working-class heroes became cocaine-class tax-exiles. By January 1968, The Who were pure vaudeville – "Smashing guitars used to be real anger; it isn't anymore. It's theatrical melodrama," said the Mod who discovered Meher Baba and had a baby called "Tommy".

The Fab Four got divorced, Eric Clapton gave up guitar-heroism for heroin and The Rolling Stones played footsie with socialites and Satan. Hope I get rich before I get old.

Meanwhile, back in the States ... garage-bands erupted like coast-to-coast acne as a new generation of crew-cuts got to first base with the black R & B and soul that the all-pervasive Brit-Beat Invasion stole its licks from originally.

True to Asian and world war form, the Americans arrived years late with an advanced state of technology. They may have been neophytes, but they could afford better equipment than anyone else.

Rock became the sole property of white dopes high on punk everywhere as bands like ? And The Mysterions, The Electric Prunes and The Magic Mushrooms came up out of nowhere and scored one hit before going straight back there. The lucky ones got jobs modelling Valderma.

This adolescent angst soundtrack was the first exposition of the trash aesthetic to get branded as "punk rock"; a revolt into anti-style consisting of a raw, basic, brazen flaunting of electric toys to pump out revenge anthems directed at the perennial Unholy Trinity of comfortable, self-contained pain-inducers – real or imagined – in the affluent lifestyle of the average white American teenage boy circa mid-Sixties; their parents, their teachers and – most of all – their girlfriends.

But oblivion beckoned; the garage-bands' enthusiastic celebration of solipsism was already dated, unfashionable and obsolete. Uncle Sam napalmed Vietnamese villages and His offspring burnt their draft cards. All across the nation, you could hear the hair grow as innocence discovered acid.

It took a Lenin to make Marx's philosophy recognisable; it took The Byrds, The Mamas And The Papas and Sonny And Cher to get Dylan on the AM playlist. Arthur Rimbaud and Woody Guthrie doing the Wall Street Shuffle hand in hand . . . they made his pop-psalms listenable and got across to an area where Dylan's influence was minimal – the singles chart.

But by this time the intelligentsia were concerned purely with albums, one eye on artistic merit and the other on bigger profits/prophets.

The Byrds never watered Dylan down but made him bearable . . . it's alright, ma, he's only whining. And Dylan learned from the Pop groups; as well as being electric, his later work was mainly boy-meets-girl with the token protest thrown in whenever he remembered. Sonny and Cher believed in the songs they sang infinitely more than Dylan ever did; the crossover product, less nitpickingly political and more humane, is invariably more sincere than dogma – and therefore has more integrity, less pretension. When The Rolling Stones were on their very first tour of the USA, they slept on the floor of Sonny and Cher's mansion.

But in Haight-Ashbury there was an epidemic – here, dropping acid was more important than moving units. "Raising of consciousness" was a luxury just the affluent could indulge in; Jimi Hendrix had black skin but was adopted by the hippies as their token Tom tab, the only black star on acid.

Hallucinogenic honkies like Jefferson Airplane, Grateful Dead, Moby Grape, Love and Captain Beefheart consumed LSD with the religious fervour of a penitent playing with rosary beads.

For the first time, rock was a vehicle for religious appetites. Even The Beach Boys had a Maharishi ("He's my Little Deuce Guru, you don't know what I got"), and everyone from The Rolling Stones to Frank Sinatra's third wife was going to Katmandu in their Kashmir sweater. Ringo may have returned from India complaining that it was "just like Butlin's" but sanity was still a long way away and Brian Epstein was being buried.

Highbrow critics weaned on the classics swooned like bobbysoxers over Sergeant Pepper's Chemical Rebellion In A Cosmic Vacuum. Cannabis sativa nestled next to savoury canapes as Hampstead hors d'oeuvres. Jimi Hendrix employed a stooge to sample every tab of acid for that pretentious little bouquet. The consumers of Alternative Product in their baubles, bangles and beads forsook surfboards and Liverpool accents for Hipperanto like "high" and "trip" ("tower block" and "dole queue" were but a twinkle in the iris of enterprising entrepreneurs not yet out of business school.) Rock had bartered its purity and vulgarity for raising of consciousness and respectability.

But even in the new aware rock and roll, the barricades were still built of papier mâché; be the first one on your block to have your boy come home in a headband! Elsewhere, the blood didn't taste of tomatoes. In Paris, left-wing students and trade unionists fought running battles with the gendarmes as the authorities desperately poured tons of cement over the instant artillery cobbled streets of the burning capital. The youth of Japan, Mexico, Greece and Germany would also have regarded the flashing of peace signs as high satire – but back in the USA, who needs unions when you've got the Mafia?

The blacks were burning Watts while the whites were burning joss-sticks, love being all you need when your idol's rich and your guru's smooth-talking. Any hint of a threat to the great American status quo was muzzled with a recording contract – it's a career man's life as a vinyl battery hen – and hitched to the corporation treadmill. Energies ostensibly committed to the annihilation of the establishment were enlisted in the lucrative perpetuation of nothing more subversive than the generation gap.

The prime example was the MC5, a Detroit band formed in 1967 by John Sinclair, "Minister of Information of the White Panther Party". Let's hear it for Mr Sinclair, as he tells you in his own words why they were formed!

"The MC5 is totally committed to the revolution. With our music and our economic genius we plunder the unsuspecting straight world for money and the means to carry out our program, and revolutionise its children at the same time. And with our entrance into the straight media we have demonstrated to the honkies that anything they do to fuck with us will be exposed to their children. You don't need to get rid of all the honkies, you just rob them of their replacements and let their breed atrophy and die out, with its heirs cheering triumphantly around it. We don't have guns yet – not all of us anyway – because we have more powerful weapons – direct access to millions of teenagers is one of our most potent, and their belief in us is another. But we will use guns if we have to – we will do anything – if we have to. We have no illusions."

Neither had Judge Colombo when he awarded Sinclair a ten-year jail sentence for passing two free marijuana cigarettes to undercover narcotic agents with their sheriff's badges pinned inside their headbands. Scolded Colombo, "He represents a person who has deliberately flaunted and scoffed at the law." He waved a hand in dismissal. "Take him away."

The MC5 themselves weren't exactly busting an alternative gut to bake good old John a hash cake with a file inside, to spring the dude and get back to the revolution. Far from it; they felt they'd paid their urbane guerrilla union dues to their sugar lump daddy Svengali with their first fab album waxing "Kick Out The Jams". Recorded live, it was a fumbling mating of screeching, headbanging Heavy Metal and fashionable politico-platitudes delivered in best/worst Billy Graham Bible-banging self-righteous rhetoric.

No sooner was their conscience buried safely behind bars than the Angry Young Businessmen obsequiously got tight with rock critic Jon "No H" Landau and smartly did an about-turn. With Landau handling production chores, the MC5 cut "Back In The USA", pure pop pap sheep-dipped in transparent raiments of youth and rebellion. They came on like bitter Monkees, chortling tinny, three-minute, wishful thinking hymns to teenage lust, sitting in the classroom at high school and fighting with cops.

But the album's title track had sounded infinitely more subversive when performed ten years previously by its cynical author Chuck Berry, a black man fresh from jail. He had handled the celebration of America with derisive humour; in the plump pink hands and mealy mouths of the MC5, "Back In The USA" sounded as superficially sincere as a holiday jingle.

To Sinclair the entire album must have sounded like a Dear John letter:–

"Then one day I had a perfect plan/I'd shake my ass and scream in a rock and roll band/From now on there'll be no compromising/Rock and roll music is the best advertising."

From inside, their ex-guiding light seethed "You guys wanted to be bigger than The Beatles and I wanted you to be bigger than Chairman Mao." Despite their desperate attempt at mass acceptance the album sold badly, not even recouping the advance Atlantic had paid them – thus gaining cult status and subsequently becoming one of the most vastly over-rated albums in the history of rock. When their third album "High Time" met the same indifferent fate, the band lost their recording contract and disappeared.

The band's lead vocalist Robin Tyner reappeared years later on a trip to England as an obese bespectacled journalist trading on past glories, who declined joints from strangers and who hefted his weighty torso onto a stage to guest with Eddie And The Hotrods before a young audience who had never heard of him.

The demise of the MC5 was indicative of the fact that in the USA the youth didn't have to be contained; just corralled, like half a million radical sheep. Out of this grew the festival phenomenon, in which the kids got it together just enough to wallow in the mud.

Monterey in June 1967 (featuring The Who, Jimi Hendrix, Janis Joplin, Brian Jones and Otis Redding) was the dress rehearsal for Woodstock, August 1969 (three days of The Who, Janis Joplin, Joan Baez, Jefferson Airplane, Grateful Dead, Crosby, Stills, Nash and Young and many more.) Love Nation show of unity; see the movie, buy the triple album! Those wonderful friends you'll remember forever!

The highway to Woodstock was clogged with an eight-mile traffic jam of car-owning hippies on their way to the fun, a freak summer thunderstorm turned the site to a quagmire of mud and – as the portable toilets overflowed – the police declared Woodstock a "disaster area".

The crowd of part-time bohemians at Woodstock was the size of a city, but the seemingly limitless supply of sex and drugs and rock and roll kept the contented kiddies too peaceful, placid and passive for any urban reality symptoms – hence the media myth of the festival as Birth Of A Nation social landmark. The gurgling inmates of Woodstock would have suffered severe spiritual starvation (it was a long walk back to Mom's apple pie) had not the local Women's Group of the Jewish Community Centre spoon-fed the Utopia frontiersmen 30,000 sandwiches, and had not Woodstock's 49-year-old dairy farmer owner Max Yasgur donated large quantities of milk and cheese. Even the outraged residents of Woodstock warmed to the helpless hippie nation when they too began to make a groovy profit out of the Aquarian Exposition.

Because the only "supermarket" on the site was a chemical Co-op selling hashish, marijuana, LSD, mescaline, psilocybin and opium. In the heat of the hedonistic goldrush to the Promised Swampland, it never occurred to the co-eds that their stomachs wouldn't be kept as full as the family freezer. For all their cunning counter-culture capitalism, the Big Daddies of Woodstock – 25-year-old Porsche-driving entrepreneur Mike Lang and 24-year-old investment concern boss John Roberts – had forgotten that man cannot live on good vibes alone. There was no food in the land of plenty.

Which left the ravenous ravers at the mercy of charitable handouts, local daylight robbers and ... now a word from our Sponsor (choke on it, suckers). Had the authorities felt at all threatened by the lumpenhippies, they would have let them eat love beads or sent in the National Guard with rubber bullets. As it was, they sent in the Air Force with 300 lbs of edible treats; despite the mounting protest against what this same army was dropping in Vietnam, the peanut-butter sure tasted swell. Manna from heaven, courtesy of President Nixon.

When the half a million campers went home after their three-day fling, the head of Monticello's constabulary was full of praise: "Notwithstanding their personality, their dress and their ideas, they are the most courteous, considerate and well-behaved group of kids I have ever been in contact with in my 24 years of police work."

The smiling benevolence with which the police stalked the half-inherent Americana, half-drug-induced polite passivity of the Woodstock playpen was paralleled by the attitude of the Hell's Angels to the non-active mass of hippies, because the fundamental philosophy of both the hated cops and the revered Angels was founded upon the evolution of mindless machismo which Gore Vidal had nailed to the Stars and Stripes as THE M3 LINE – when Woodstock ended, Sharon Tate had been dead for seven days.

"There has been from Henry Miller to Norman Mailer to Charles Manson a logical progression. The Miller-Mailer-Manson "man" (or M3 for short) has been conditioned to think of women as, at best, breeders of sons, at worst, objects to be poked, humiliated, killed … M3 was born, emigrated to America, killed Indians, killed blacks, conned women … righteous murder stalks the land."

Though the cops/Angels tolerated the hippies who opted out of the M3 brotherhood in favour of all-round euphoric apathy, both the boys in blue and the boys on bikes screamed in vehement panic at the activist minority of anti-war demonstrators, who had realised that no revolution was won by sitting stoned in a field.

Despite this, the reactionary rednecks on sparkling Harleys were elevated to folk-hero status by such counter-culture luminaries as acid-testing dilettante Ken "Cuckoo Nest" Kesey and moronic marathon-rockers The Grateful Dead – all the hip guys love a bike-boy – whose leader Jerry Garcia provided references for the Angels when The Rolling Stones at the climax of a box-office smash-hit American tour decided to play a massive free festival to grab the top rock-hero rung, open to offers due to The Beatles being in the painful throes of divorce proceedings and Bob Dylan playing the part of hermit family-man.

For The Rolling Stones wanted no establishment "pigs" at the Californian speedway of Altamont, just outside San Francisco – they would provide their own alternative police force. It was fitting that The Stones, who with their myriad celebratory dabblings in Satanism, mindless violence, dirty hypodermic needles and other habits which were the direct antithesis of love, peace and tolerance, should choose to replace one crew of law-enforcers with another of even greater brutality. The doublethink was ripe for violent nemesis.

In the last month of the last year of the Sixties, 300,000 people hooked down the depression cocktail of downers and cheap wine and set fire to mountains of garbage to fend off the freezing winter air as they huddled on the bleak hills around the Altamont speedway. The Hell's Angels had been paid $500 worth of beer for keeping the peace.

By the time Santana, the first act of the festival, were onstage, the Angels were already brutalising the audience. In front of the stage a young man was repeatedly kicked in the face and the set was interrupted by another Angel rushing across the stage to beat up someone else. When Jefferson Airplane played, guitarist Marty Balin was knocked senseless by a pool-cue wielding Angel for having the audacity to intervene in one of the many beatings being handed out by the Angels.

In complete control, the Angels drove their bikes straight through the packed crowd to park them by the side of the stage. At the end of Crosby, Stills, Nash And Young's set, a horde of stretchers were sent into the audience and came back carrying bloodied, unconscious bodies to the first aid tent.

After a lengthy delay, The Stones themselves appeared and found themselves confined to a minute stage area surrounded by the jeering, openly contemptuous Angels who found a source of great mirth in Mick Jagger's dancing. As The Stones' third number "Sympathy For The Devil" ground to a halt, a group of Hell's Angels some ten yards from the stage stabbed to death a young black man named Meredith Hunter, who had offended the Angels by attending the festival with his girlfriend who happened to be very pretty, very blonde and very white.

They made a movie of it, of course, in which Mick Jagger wept as he watched a video-tape slow-motion instant-replay of the murder and Keith Richard (whose cocaine bill after one 49-date US tour was a quarter of a million dollars) demonstrated considerably less compassion.

"People were just asking for it . . . all those nude, fat people. They had victims' faces."

"The kids are being hyped," Lou Reed had said before Altamont, on peace and love versus his "realism". Reed and The Velvet Underground were exponents of twisted black East Coast pessimism in the face of flowery West Coast optimism, both loathed and feared by the hippies. Lou Reed had met John Cale in New York City, 1964, and The Velvet Underground were formed after making a big impression on Andy Warhol and his menagerie. The Velvets made their debut at the Mixed Media Exploding Plastic Inevitable show in 1966 and their first album appeared a year later, brimming with paeans to urban paranoia, smack glorification and sado-masochism. Failing to achieve chart placings, the nihilists pursued solo careers. From Detroit, also pretending to destroy themselves before anyone else could, came Iggy And The Stooges. James Jewel Osterberg a.k.a. lead singer Iggy Stooge achieved notoriety and a recording contract not so much by his warbling – he and his anonymous band were still hungover with sporadic attacks of doomy post-Doors mystical acid gloom which they dropped on their second album in favour of Iggy's patented routine of self-hate, self-abuse and self-degradation – as for urging the crowd to buy shares in his crucifixion.

Iggy's party-pieces included – dousing his body in burning wax! Swan-diving onto broken glass! Ripping his chest open with a broken bottle! Smashing his teeth through his gums with the micro-phone and crooning "The Shadow Of Your Smile"! Covering his body in peanut butter!

"Basically I'm a nurd," Iggy told the authors in late 1977. "Look at my face, it's Alfred E. Neuman."

Alfie gave the authors the shits, metaphorically. The authors gave Alfie the shits, literally. The day he minced into their office to ponce drugs, he was given a generous supply of laxatives. He gulped them greedily, causing the Mighty Poop (as we affectionately refer to him) to interrupt his gigs for the next 48 hours. Basically, he was a turd – and, as such, Born to Run.

He was racist and sexist, the hippie ideology seen through a microscope instead of rose-tinted shades. When The Stooges dissolved Iggy turned whore and later committed himself to a sanatorium.

Really, both Iggy and Lou were just flamboyant closet-cases fronting amateur-hour wimp bands, the members of which would have been just as happy if they'd done acid-drops and "believed" in love and peace. Though, significantly, Haight-Ashbury was eventually destroyed by a soul-sucking plague of heroin – Alfred E. Iggy and Loopy Lou's own particular hype.

"Because it makes me feel like I'm a man/When I stick a spike into my vein", from The Velvet Underground's "Heroin" summed up both Lou and Iggy most succinctly. This odd couple were to be *the* Sixties legacy to the next generation, though wearing needles in one's arm was just as much an affectation as sporting flowers in one's coiffure . . . it just sounded more drastic on plastic.

The funky junkie duo would have languished in obscurity, growing evermore fat, flaccid and forgotten, had it not been for the cataclysmic David Bowie. "The Rise And Fall Of Ziggy Stardust And The Spiders From Mars" was Bowie's third album, released in the summer of 1972. Set five years before Doomsday, against a back-drop of Brave New World escapism, its naive obsession with Space Age Science Fantasy – blatantly displayed in songs like "Moonage Daydream", "Starman", "Lady Stardust", "Star" and "Ziggy Stardust" – reflected the resignation of a generation who had washed their hands of Earth after their failure to create a new world during their weekend picnic at Yasgur's farm.

Appealing to Bowie's own mid-twenties contemporaries who had converted to all things sci-fi after abandoning belief in mere mortals, and to a new generation of teenagers too young to know or care about the past glories of the leftover idols and restless for an icon of their own, "Ziggy Stardust" was a camp novelette starring ex-mime artiste Bowie in the title role of rock star as leper messiah consumed by his ego.

Showing considerable integrity, a good business head and a dramatic sense of timing, Bowie revealed in an interview that he was bisexual, setting a precedent in the tight-lipped world of show-business. Although bands such as Alice Cooper – standard Heavy Metal muzak fronted by the baby-doll-beheading fat ham Alice himself – T. Rex – androgynous imp singing purple prose juke-box classics – and Slade – platform-boot stomping would-be working-class heroes – had been around since the start of the decade, it took someone as intelligent and glamorous as Bowie to instigate the pop renaissance soon categorised as Glitter Rock, with exponents as diverse as Gary Glitter, Alvin Stardust and Sweet – chicken-in-a-basket brickie cabaret and hod-carriers in gold lamé hotpants – Elton John and Roy Wood – fat old Tin Pan Alley tune-smith tarts in more mascara than anyone since Dusty Springfield – Queen and Cockney Rebel – competent rock bands *ordinaire* fronted by portentous, preening, piss-pot bards – and Roxy Music, whose first and second albums contain the only truly timeless rock music ever recorded, and were infinitely more convincing in their themes of alienation than Bowie playing Captain Kirk to his lead guitarist's Mr Spock. Roxy Music, alas, ended not with a bang but with a simper when Bryan Ferry subsequently joined the afore-mentioned piss-pot parade.

By 1973, Bowie was influential enough to take his poor relations Iggy and Lou out of mothballs and serve them up for Seventies con-sumption. He produced Reed's limp-wristed self-parody "Transfor-mer" and Iggy's vinyl tout "Raw Power" and was left at the altar on both occasions when Iggy and Lou flounced back across the Atlantic to resume their romance with heroin. Ungrateful bitches!

At least they were spared the soporific musical diet of Hip Easy Listening, Disco Fodder and Heavy Metal which had drenched young earbuds before Glitter Rock and regained its stranglehold by

1975. All three products matched the mood of economic crisis depression prevalent in a UK torn by one million plus unemployed and legions of school-leavers swelling their ranks every day, the three-day week, teeming assembly-line education and the Tory mis-rule culminating in miners' strike black-outs.

Coffee-table credibility Hip Easy Listening was an insipid aural palliative for and by jaundiced hippies of all ages and social standing, with the artiste as creator of product and his worth measured on the *Financial Times* index. Disco Fodder was mechanical, mindless, sanitised soul, in which Uncle Tom sported an Afro to provide the staple dancing ration of the nation's youth whose lives were similarly mass-produced; it was the perfect backdrop for a slipshod education running the line to the factory, office or dole. *Top Of The Pops* played colonial host to a regular stream of nimble-toed melon chompers. Disco was the opiate of the prole – agent of social order, it featured no polemics beyond get down and boogie, party, party and Dating Do's And Don'ts.

The epic Teutonic anaesthetic, Heavy Metal was brutally ham-fisted renderings of blues-based white rock – a totally moronic and downered wipe-out which complimented the Seventies teenage leisure activities of arson and alcoholism.

The emergence of Pub Rock in 1975 was a reaction against the giant stadiums at which the opulent rock aristocracy occasionally deigned to play, and against the slumming matrons who were getting backstage passes – Elizabeth Taylor with The Who and Princess Margaret with The Rolling Stones. The Pub Rock backlash was re-vamped R & B cranked out in small sweaty venues who had taken to serving live music along with the brown ale.

Mostly, the music itself was dire and derivative (a fact easily overlooked by a pub of pilchard-packed punters, pissed as newts) and, even with record company financial enthusiasm fired by trade press critical hyperbole, few Pub Rock bands transcended the rock 'n' bitter scene and moved on to greater things – the major problem being their inability to capture the live gig excitement on cold, hard, vinylised plastic.

But despite the demise of the Pub Rock ethos – which had always been strictly confined to the capital – the venues created by the aural movement remained and grass-roots rock combos had a ready made gig-circuit training ground in London for their lean years of apprenticeship. It was no longer uncool for a band to climb on stage without a P.A. system the size of a Lassky's warehouse. In New York City, the club scene had been thriving for some time and had spawned a dead-on-arrival disaster-area outfit calling themselves The New York Dolls, who by 1975 had achieved the popularity of acne-blitzed transvestite lepers addicted to heroin.

Formed in Babylon two years previously, The Dolls were the most blatant Rolling Stones rip-off of all time though paradoxically exuding ten times more nerve-bruising belligerent excitement than Mick and Keith's ritzy old tarts had ever mustered.

The New York Dolls starred tousled blond David JoHansen on lead vocals and audience-baiting, an ex-teenage pornlette who had graced such celluloid evergreens as *Studs On Main Street* and *Bike Boys Go Ape*. He danced like a white James Brown in chiffon and stilettoes flanked by rhythm guitarist Sylvain Sylvain, a man-handled Manhattan marionette with corkscrew curls, and lead guitarist Johnny Thunders, a back-combed brunette baseball jock turned junk rock starlet. As befitted a good Italian boy who loved his mother, Johnny would *always* execute a neat reverse duck-walk for the sheltered privacy of the amplifiers whenever gripped with a new wave of nausea. Bassist Arthur Kane resembled a giant haystack turned hooker turned Bowery bum paralysed by paraffin while drummer Jerry "Atric" Nolan looked like the sulky substitute he was, drafted in to The Dolls' rancid ranks after their original drummer Billy Murcia committed soap-skidding unintentional suicide after tarrying too long in the tub with a bottle of booze and a mountain of Mandrax.

Unrepentant poseurs, The Dolls wanted to be stars because there was nothing else left to be. Incompetent musicians, they owed more to Marilyn Monroe than to Elvis Presley, raking over the ashes of the living dead with their Famous Dopes On Opiates fashion-consciousness. On stage, JoHansen, Sylvain and Thunders raged around like crowd-conscious beauty queens with hostile possums housed down their G-strings (just to obtain that impressive *bulge*, one understands), frequently colliding and toppling off their rhinestoned cowboy platforms, their three-minute masterpieces of solipsistic sleaze such as "Pills", "Trash" and "Personality Crisis" very much the icing on the fairy cake.

Due to their self-imposed handicaps – Thunders and Nolan addicted to heroin and Arthur Kane a chronic alcoholic – and despite their recording contract with Mercury, their reputation as unreliable degenerates made it practically impossible for them to get a gig anywhere outside of Max's Kansas City. However, during a disastrous European tour they made such an impression on a tone-deaf East End tailor with a business in Chelsea that he followed The Dolls to Paris and later to New York and eventually became their manager. He tried to prevent the band coming apart at the seams, even working as a window-cleaner to supplement their income, re-launching them in threads of red leather before a huge hammer-and-sickle flag.

But neither the audience nor The Dolls took it seriously and the band began to disintegrate. During a residence in Florida, hard-won by the hustler acting as their manager, pin-cushion pair Thunders and Nolan escaped back to New York where they formed The Heartbreakers. Within two weeks The New York Dolls' erstwhile manager was back in his King's Road shop.

But the draper's potential had not bypassed the eagle eye of Johnny Thunders.

"Malcolm McLaren is the greatest con-man that I ever met."

# SEX

Oh bondage, up mine!

Before Malcolm McLaren and his partner Vivienne Westwood had discovered *Sex*, they had placed their faith in England's dwindling tribe of Teddy Boy fossils as the most potent means of challenging society's established standards and prejudices. In 1971 their shop at 430 King's Road, Chelsea, had sold facsimiles of original Teddy Boy drapes, drainpipes, bootlace ties, luminous socks and brothel creepers under the name *Let It Rock*.

It took McLaren and Westwood two years to discover what any kid within spitting distance of the street would have taken for granted; that the staid and settled Teds were duck's-ass reactionaries, sexist, racist and suspicious of a change in the weather. But McLaren – a professional art-school-attender of eight years standing and dabbler in stage-design, educated beyond all instinct – and Westwood – a primary teacher, mother and *hausfrau* prior to being swept off her Scholl's by her flame-haired Bohemian – were only 30-plus (they had a lot to learn) and were convinced of the mystic qualities inherent in a pair of crepe-layered beetle-crushers. With the realisation that they had been barking up the wrong cult and that the Teddy Boys were "not at all what we thought they were", the disillusioned dilettantes transferred their allegiance to the leather-clad rockers, re-naming their shop in honour of the legend emblazoned across a biker's back, *Too Fast To Live, Too Young To Die*. But the zoot suits, chains and fringes were another dead-end.

By now, McLaren and Westwood had gleaned sufficient experience of the working world which existed outside of their sheltered theories to realise that the generation gap would never get their names on the front of the Sunday papers, let alone shake the foundations of civilisation. After a radical reconsideration of shock tactics, they hit upon *Sex* as the ultimate bastion of public inhibition and outrage.

Their creations flaunted the subject matter of surreptitious plain brown wrapper titillation *not* to cater for the secret desires of guilt-ridden respectable perverts but to shock indifferent and dismissive elders into white-knuckled, cardiac-arrest indignance. *Sex* output included T-shirts bearing extracts of hard-core porn prose and numerous pictorial depravities, a full range of rubberwear and bondage trousers tied together at the knee.

None of these clothes were either designed or worn to make the customer look alluring; on the contrary, the flagrant fashion in which the clothes used sex as an offensive weapon required a certain asexuality on the part of the wearer. They used sex not to entice but to horrify, the perfect expression of which was found in Jordan "Don't Call Me Pamela" Hook, the *Sex* salesgirl who wore cutaway-buttock plastic leotards with black suspender belt and thigh boots while striving to make her hair, face and body as puke-promptingly repulsive as possible. The tag-team of tailors at last attracted the wild youth they had always been sniffing after as Fleet Street pounced and the press-clippings for the *Sex* scrapbook kept coming even faster than the bricks jilted Teds playfully passed to their Uncle Mal through the shop window.

*Sex* business busting out all over, Malcolm felt the need to conquer fresh fields and past-times new, investing a purseful of ill-gotten pee in a course of singing lessons. But the neophyte night-ingale's warbling ceased when his justifiable age-paranoia made him see sense; instead, he consoled himself with the vicarious satisfaction of overseeing the plodding progress of a group of seventeen-year-old ex-skinhead *Sex* regulars who called them-selves The Swankers and were the proud owners of an entire P.A. system plus instruments stolen piece by piece over a period of two years.

The boys had been using *Sex* as a Fagin's lair ever since they started picking P.A.s partly because of McLaren's predilection for using his shop assistants and customers as stage props and partly because he was the only adult who actively encouraged them to pursue an alternative to their pre-planned existence.

The Swankers' roll-call comprised Glen Matlock on bass, an art student and unashamed Paul McCartney fan who worked weekends in *Sex* – the most accomplished musician in the band which wasn't saying much; former drummer Steve "Heterosexual" Jones on vocals and Spanish waiter imitations; electrician's mate Paul Cook as the band's strong and silent drummer after picking up paradiddles from his best friend Steve; and on guitar, the enigma known as Wally, a buck-toothed bespectacled liability whose legendary ugliness has since achieved mythical status matched only by Medusa's.

As the only Swankers who knew their quavers from their crotchets, Matlock and Wally called the tunes regarding the band's rehearsal repertoire – wrinkled Sixties power-pap such as the floral gibberish of The Foundations' "Build Me Up Buttercup", the transient chastity of Love Affair's "A Day Without Love", the crocodile corn of The Rolling Stones "As Tears Go By" and the santised Mod compromise of early Small Faces and Who jingles. Cook and Jones mourned The New York Dolls with dewy-eyed Amateur Hour empathy in vain until Malcolm McLaren moved in with a vengeance, projecting his vision of *the* supremely subversive rock band onto the blank generation pages of The Swankers.

A self-conscious performer, Steve Jones was given a guitar to hide behind and improved so rapidly that soon the band were able to relieve themselves of their Achilles eyesore. As Wally swanked off into the sunset, McLaren baptised his lewd brood The Sex Pistols; imagery contrived to strike treble terror into the hearts of the slack-jawed public – fucking, violence and an advertisement for Malcolm's shop.

Steve Jones's habit of sitting out certain chords caused Paul Cook to consider following in Wally's footsteps unless a second guitarist was added. They auditioned Steve New and it was love at first sight – barely fifteen, decked out in Kensington Market tack and looking like he put all his pocket-money up his nose. As an added bonus he could even play his guitar. But Steve refused to play Samson to Malcolm's Delilah and was instructed to pistol off when he declined a trip to the barber's for his shoulder-length barnet to be clipped to regulation Vaseline-spiked peroxide crop.

Fully appreciating how precariously close The Sex Pistols had come to gaining a Steve New and losing a Steve Shopsoiled, S. Jones started going to bed with just his *Bert Weedon's Teach Yourself Guitar Book*, and the girls had to wait till he wielded a more fluid plectrum before the neighbourhood pushover was back in circulation.

Jones began developing from fat-zero to axe-hero after one easy lesson but although he possessed the front of a confidence man it was patently obvious he lacked the confidence required of a front-man and McLaren began searching for a suitably iconoclastic focal point. He knew exactly the qualifications he was looking for – "a lunatic".

During a brief sojourn north of the border up Glasgow way to unload musical equipment still piping hot off the back of a lorry, Malcolm espied from his parked car a good-looking young jock who didn't have long hair and didn't wear flares skulking out of a guitar shop. McLaren was attended in the car by ex-used-motor salesman, *Sex* shop printer and all purpose underling Bernie Rhodes, who Malcolm promptly instructed to act as balding retriever and approach the youth with an offer he'd probably refuse.

Rhodes accosted the youth and asked him if he wanted to be in a band. Midge Ure of Salvation (soon to be re-named Slik) replied that he was already spoken for but Rhodes persuaded him to go over to the car and listen to the proposition of his red-haired master. Mal couldn't sell Midge a place in The Sex Pistols, only a stolen amplifier.

Back in London, Steve Jones told McLaren to keep his eyes

peeled for a teenaged amphetamine hunchback with green hair and rotted dentures to match, seen some six months ago haunting the dark shadows of *Sex*. The gods grinned on Malcolm, for John Lydon of Finsbury Park slouched into *Sex* right on cue and zing went the strings of Malcolm's bondage pants.

Mal licked lascivious lips when he clocked the likely lad's sadistically mutilated Pink Floyd T-shirt with the words I HATE scribbled in a biro trembling with furious loathing above the Dodo's moniker. John was not a pretty sight; when Mother Nature was handing out the good looks he'd been at the back of the queue, and by the time he'd got to the counter all She had left was meningitis, weak eyes, teeth held together by steel rods, stunted growth and a permanent sinus. He also boasted to having had the pick of the piles, which he claimed dangled down his inside legs and required frequent pruning with a razor-blade.

O.K. – so he was no oil-painting, but he looked a regular Beau Brummel when he shambled down the street in his Sunday best, safety-pins holding together his tasty Oxfam threads, spitting on any passing hippie as he wandered to confession whistling an Irish jig.

Possibly smelling a casting couch, Lydon responded to McLaren's initial advances with surly derision, but was enticed through the portals of a nearby tavern when Malcolm discovered that the quickest way to Lydon's heart was through a can of lager. Supping gratis Heineken, Lydon hid behind his protective shield of suspicious hostility excess, giving McLaren and the boys a pistol-whipping with the thrashing machine of his well-oiled tongue.

But his mocking insults only intensified the desire of Mal's press-gang to enlist this new kid in *Sex* into their under-staffed ranks. Lydon held out for sixty minutes before returning to the shop with his prospective employers for an informal audition (his performing debut) miming to Alice Cooper's "School's Out" in front of the *Sex* juke-box.

The spectacle was more side-splitting than awe-inspiring, but sufficiently hypnotic to totally convince Mal's crew that here was the hysterical beacon they had dreamed of for so long. When Lydon agreed to join the band McLaren recognised that the goose had laid a golden egg, and he seized it by the throat volunteering to act as full-time manager of The Sex Pistols and having a contract drawn up and signed just to make everything nice and legally official.

Lydon came close to deserting when he was the only member of the band to turn up for their first rehearsal, and the offended stray was only hounded back into the flock after much pleading and wheedling from McLaren and the boys – "We mean it most sincerely, John."

Mollified, John returned to rehearsals like a conquering hero and got down to writing a set of lyrics which made The New York Dolls look like Mormons who weren't into bondage. Civilised by Matlock's melodies, songs such as "Seventeen":

– "You're only 29, you've got a lot to learn/But when your business dies, you will not return/We don't care about long hair/I don't wear flares/I don't work, I just speed/That's all I need/I'm a lazy sod" – "Satellite" – "Trying to join the scene but you're too obscene/You're looking like a big fat pink baked bean/How do you figure that you'd be any use/When all you're gonna get is my abuse/You know I don't like where you come from/It's just a satellite of London" – "No Future" – "God save the Queen/A fascist regime/It made you a moron/A potential H-bomb/God save the Queen/She ain't no human being/There is no future in England's dreaming"

– and "Anarchy In The UK" (actually written by Jamie Reid, a "socially aware" side-kick of McLaren's) –

"I am an Anti-Christ/I am an anarchist/Don't know what I want but I know how to get it/I wanna destroy passers-by/Cos I wanna be anarchy/No dogsbody"

– were the basis of their first gig at St Martin's College of Art in November 1975, supporting a rock 'n' roll revival band.

Led by Johnny Rotten (a name coined by Paul Cook's mum when she saw the state of Lydon's teeth), The Sex Pistols were showered with bottles, inspiring vigilante outrage in both Teds and students – two threatened tribes sharing a staid fear of upheaval. The crowd were appeased when a plug was pulled out and The Sex Pistols set was abruptly terminated.

For three months The Pistols crashed any venue gullible enough to let them set up their equipment onstage, and soon they had attracted a hard-core following known as the Bromley Contingent; a posse of unrepentant poseurs committed to attaining fame despite their paucity of any talent other than being noticed. They achieved their aim by displaying themselves in a manner meticulously calculated to kill – Technicolor hair, the latest *Sex* modes and faces painted with the instinctive skill of the truly obsessed. They were Sue Catwoman, Steve Havoc, Siouxsie Sioux, Helen, Debbie, and Nils, the latter of whom turned his cronies green with envy when he landed a gig as co-manager of The Sex Pistols – though soon cut down by McLaren to the band's personal assistant.

In February 1976 an ugly but affluent figure from McLaren's arty past raised its head. It was Andrew Logan, sculpting socialite with a penchant for surrounding himself with the most expensive and extensive collection of decorative human trash-cans currently reflecting the capital's fashionable malaise. His annual celebrations of decay have included a Miss World parody in which a horde of trans-sexuals tout their trophies, a favourite with all the other freaks. But for this year's entertainment, drag-queens were ditched in favour of vital young yobbos.

Between greedily guzzling the buckshee booze and attempting to steal Logan's pricey pretty pictures, The Pistols played a trio of sets comprising their patented noise for napalming the psyche of a nation, blowing the jaded cocaine-set menagerie out of their boredom chic. It could have been a comic-strip – Studied Decadence meets Social Disease.

Prior to The Sex Pistols' party-piece, Logan's gormless gourmets had experienced everything twice and been bored to death the first time – the very reason why McLaren had chosen them as the Lazarus guinea-pigs to Rotten's Anti-Christ. Shocked back to life, they scurried off to their grapevines to spread the faith. The Sex Pistols' fate was sealed.

Logan's set may have kidded themselves into believing they had developed cold-blooded indifference into a fine art, but they merely reflected the apathy prevalent throughout every stratum of class, age and wealth in the dulled sensibilities of the entire nation. Which made them just as vulnerable to the real *rage* of The Sex Pistols as Appalled of Cheam.

Their fury made them innovators; for the first time a band was directly reacting against the music business monolith, and if they sounded disgusted, demented, destructive and depressed with the sordid planet and everything on it, then it was certainly what was needed to inflict scorched earth policy prior to the deluge of the new wave.

Rock had always flirted with violence as mere metaphor; Rotten destroyed the pose, and replaced it with the reality – constantly haranguing the audience with streams of abuse, spitting and snarling lyrics as though they tasted of his own piles, dancing like a rotting corpse still shaking from snaring its yarbles on the lid of a closing coffin, glassy eyes burning, pallid flesh decorated with self-inflicted fag-burns, amphetamine-parched lips turned back in savage contempt as he went for the jugular – sometimes literally.

The Pistols had crystallised widespread repression, giving it form, style and direction. Single-handed, they had instigated a movement. Kids began finding each other, with Pistols gigs as the rallying flag and new bands started scuffling for any equipment they could lay their greasy paws on as the whole thing got off the ground.

Banned for hostilities provoked at the Nashville and Marquee, The Sex Pistols eventually secured a residency at Oxford Street's 100 Club. By that summer, Punk Rock had evolved to the stage where it would be officially recognised by the rock establishment as a genuine new order (even if few journalists/record company executives/club owners considered it more appealing than small-pox), and in September The 100 Club played host to a two-day Punk Festival. Both nights represented Punk's Deb's Coming Out Ball. The scene was a new height of funtime exhibitionism with the mandatory pose of menace the first day, when The Pistols topped, giving the club the oppressive sulphate-tension of a football terrace. On the last night the pose exploded into tragic reality; The Damned baited hecklers and got a glass thrown at them. It missed its target and shattered against a wooden post, blinding an 18-year-old girl in one eye. The tragedy tarnished the entire movement with one brush in the Established Order's mind although the sub-sequent outraged publicity resulted in the cold irony of punk rock catapulting to Capitalist Corporate Structure Commercial Viability.

The 100 Club banned all punk acts but within a month Malcolm had found his boys a good home – The Sex Pistols signed a £40,000 recording contract with EMI.

"What a fucking dump", sneered Rotten the first time he slunk into the offices of that Monday Club of record labels.

"If you don't like it you can fuck off", snarled an EMI career-man.

They took it from there.

# PISTOLS

On 26 November 1976, the cold black copies of "Anarchy In The UK" poured off the presses and it was the greatest youth frustration anthem ever released. Just over three minutes of blind raging fury, pushing rock's perennial demonic possession stance to totally unprecedented extremes, a singularly unpretentious/working-class de-mystification, beautiful, blistering, nerve-bruising paean to anarchy as self-rule that The Sex Pistols put into off-hand obstreperous practice when they appeared liver than Bill Grundy could ever be on ITV's prime-time *Today* show and became a household name in just under three minutes.

When The Sex Pistols and a few select fans were settled opposite Grundy after a brief film-clip of the lads in action, Bill began playing verbal footsie with Siouxsie Sioux, a waitress from Chislehurst. Still basking in the alcoholic after-glow of the Thames Television "hospitality room", The Pistols responded with single-minded glee.

"You dirty sod! You dirty old man!"

"You dirty bastard!"

"You dirty fucker!"

"What a fucking rotter!"

It was the greatest response ever to the fumbling fiasco of an old man trying to chat up a young girl. As The Pistols and their fans laughed into his face, a red-faced Grundy squirmed inside his suit and tie and turned to the camera; "Well that's it for tonight. The other rocker Eamonn, I'm saying nothing else about him, will be back tomorrow. I'll be seeing you soon." He turned to the youngsters. "I hope I'm not seeing you again." He turned back to the camera, the only eye not crinkled in laughter. "From me though, goodnight."

The repressed hysteria of a nation found an outlet in John, Paul, Steve, Glen and Grundy: "The filth and the fury! Uproar as viewers jam phones! When the air turned blue! The filthiest language heard on British television! One man so furious he kicked in his £380 colour TV! 'It blew up and I was knocked backwards but I was so angry and disgusted with this filth that I took a swing with my boot! I can swear as well as anyone, but I don't want this sort of muck coming into my home at teatime! I'm not a violent person but I would like to have got hold of Grundy! He should be sacked for encouraging this sort of disgusting behaviour!'" *Daily Mirror*, 2 December 1976.

"Were The Pistols loaded? Punk Rock group 'plied with booze'!

Two-week ban on Grundy over 'filthy' show!" *The Sun*, 2 December 1976.

"Swearing is banned at home, says Mrs Grundy!" *Daily Mail*, 2 December 1976.

"Surely a button can be pressed to stop this filthy language!" *Daily Telegraph*, 2 December 1976.

Grundy was reprimanded and suspended for a fortnight by Director of Programmes Jeremy Isaacs for "inexcusably sloppy journalism", a companion ban for the long-standing exile from his local pub. The only quotes Fleet Street got from him were more expletives deleted.

Paul Cook's mother had kicked him out of his home but it didn't matter much because The Pistols were about to embark on their nationwide "Anarchy Tour". Fleet Street's screaming denunciations were frightening local councils, universities and The Rank Leisure Group – who together monopolised the country's live rock and roll venues – into embarking on a policy of banning punk rock out of existence, and had scared American band The Ramones into pulling out of the tour. Co-starring with The Pistols were The Clash, The Heartbreakers and The Damned, the latter replaced by The Buzzcocks after just one date owing to their tendency for licking any authoritarian anus.

The first gig, scheduled for 3 December at the University of East Anglia was cancelled to protect "public safety" and the students' barricades were broken down before bedtime. The next day in Derby The Pistols failed to turn up for a watch-dog audition by the Derby Borough Council Leisure Committee and a spokesman for the councillors said the band had been given a "fair chance". Back at their hotel, a girl from the *News Of The World* buzzed her editor with a hot scoop: "I got six lines of obscenities out of Rotten before he fucked off!"

The first gig not blown out was played at Leeds Polytechnic on 6 December. Anonymous in long hair, leather coat and flares among the crowd of hostile students aiming missiles at The Pistols' faces was a hack from a London evening commuter brain-candy rag dispatched with instructions from his editor to write a "front page hatchet job". He had all the relevant data he needed when Rotten dedicated "Anarchy In The UK" to a Leeds councillor, Bill Grundy and the Queen together with a colourful invitation to attempt the anatomically impossible.

The next day EMI held their Annual General Meeting; they hadn't had so much to chat about since The Beatles, MBE, had confessed to smoking dope in the Queen's carsey – as if not offering Lizzie a toke was such a big deal! Waggling a warning finger, Sir John Read said "Whether EMI releases any more of The Sex Pistols records will have to be very carefully considered."

After alleged drinkin', spittin' and vomitin' at Heathrow Airport en route to an Amsterdam gig and "Anarchy" reaching the Top Thirty, EMI melted down all existing copies of the single and dropped the band, due mainly to pressure from groups as diverse as factory workers taking strike action in protest against packing the record, ageing artistes on the label smelling a young threat and irate shareholders concerned that the controversy would make their units fall. By 25 January the "Anarchy" tour was cancelled with just five out of a prospective 20 dates played, but the jilted reprobates still had £50,000 maintenance courtesy of old flames EMI to go home to.

Despite instigating the Grundy cuss-in, being the catchy songsmith craftsman responsible for lifting The Pistols music out of an indifferent Heavy Metal quagmire and providing a melodic backdrop to Rotten's relentless sneer, Glen Matlock's love of pre-Sergeant Pepper pop had tarred him with a Young Tory brush.

Since the impressionable age of fourteen, Matlock had worked for McLaren at weekends and within a year had been introduced to Cook and Jones by the curly clothes-cutter. Incorporating the youthful enthusiasm of Paul and Steve, and the arty suss of McLaren, Matlock was the missing link who acted as interpreter – "Steve and Paul had all this equipment around and they didn't know what to do with it, so they might as well learn to play it."

Right from the beginning half of the band had been nothing more than visually acceptable labourers, but by the time The Sex Pistols achieved international notoriety, Rotten needed to be the only person McLaren would confide in, consult or question when considering the band's next move. Intelligent, articulate and – worst of all – once very close to Malcolm, Matlock was reviled by Rotten for his middle-class mummy's boy roots, ego-tripping lust for power and his mop-top allergy to Rotten's improvised nihilism. By March 1977, Glen was an ex-Pistol, usurped by John "Sid Vicious" Beverley, Rotten's bike-chain wielding chum from college. His arrival affirmed The Pistols ultra-violent reputation and resumed the friendship which had gone into abeyance when Rotten joined the band. "When I first met Vicious was when John was still deciding whether he was gonna join The Pistols or not. Rotten and Vicious were very close at that point ... Rotten used to bring him along when we met in some boozer to talk about the band", said Glen Matlock. "They were really close mates, and after John joined the band Rotten didn't see so much of Vicious because now he had The Pistols. Vicious used to be ringing him up all the time and Rotten just used to take the piss outa Vicious, really put him down and I think that Sid felt a bit left out ... and that's when Sid started beating people up".

On 9 March A & M, the label most unlikely to, signed The Sex

Pistols outside Buckingham Palace, for the benefit of the press. Rotten and Vicious celebrated the deal by beating up Paul Cook in the back of the limo that chauffeured them to their reception at A & M's office, where malicious rumour alleged A & M employees were horrified by The Pistols unique way of making themselves feel at home by spitting out wine on the Cyril Lord carpet on discovering it not to their liking, depositing fresh excrement in the in-trays, breaking a window, breaking a toilet and approaching secretaries with lewd propositions. "We at A & M are excited by The Sex Pistols", said the company's managing director Derek Green through gritted teeth.

Two days later Johnny Rotten was fined £40 for possessing amphetamine sulphate and in the small hours of the next morning encountered DJ Bob Harris and his sound engineer at London's plush poseurie The Speakeasy Club. The jockey and his pal alleged that The Pistols' party had enquired when Harris intended to play the band's new single and then assaulted them with fists and glasses leaving the DJ cut and bruised and the sound engineer in need of fourteen stitches.

Men of honour such as Rick Wakeman, Peter Frampton and Karen Carpenter were outraged by this breach of Queensberry rules and ran whining to Big Daddy A & M to make the horrid boys go away. Back at HQ The Pistols caused yet more consternation when they submitted their advertisement plans for the new single "God Save The Queen"; designed to make the boldest corgi scamper into its kennel, the ad depicted a tiaraed Queenie blindfolded with the song's title, gagged by the band's name and sporting a safety pin through that noble nose.

The events of the action-packed week since the band's signing to A & M led Derek Green to the conclusion that offering The Sex Pistols a home had been a disastrous mistake that had to be rectified immediately and at any cost. A & M destroyed 25,000 copies of "God Save The Queen" and gave The Sex Pistols the elbow, their best wishes and £75,000.

After collecting £125,000 from terminated contracts, The Pistols were untouchable – they had no label, they had no venue (just two unscheduled gigs at Leicester Square's Notre Dame Hall and Islington's Screen On The Green cinema, both publicised by conspiratorial word of mouth) and after two months in the wilderness, The Sex Pistols suffered the most inflammatory and inaccurate public excution to date when the London *Evening News* of 7 May blared the headline "Rock's Swastika Revolution!" accompanied by a large picture of The Pistols. The paper was forced to choke on an apology when McLaren rapped their knuckles by proxy:

"Dear Sir, I would like to point out that The Sex Pistols are not into any political party, least of all the loathsome National Front. I think it is extraordinarily irresponsible and dumb to give that scummy organisation a load of free publicity by connecting them with us."

The Sex Pistols finally found another label on 13 May when they became Virgin's and "God Save The Queen" was finally let loose on a world of chain-store, TV and radio bans. It was the fastest-selling single of Jubilee year, selling two million copies and reaching its Top Twenty apex in Jubilee week itself (its mercurial rise up the BBC's charts mysteriously terminated at the number two spot). The Pistols celebrated their Silver Disc on Silver Anniversary Day with a private party on board the *Queen Elizabeth* as the boat cruised down the Thames. After three hours the vessel passed the Houses of Parliament and The Pistols began playing a set up on the poop-deck. Over-excited photographers crowded ridiculously close to the band and a brief fight ensued between a protective Pistols comrade and a volatile French lens-man. The boat's owner panicked and radioed for the River Police to eject the party from his "licensed premises". Eight police launches escorted the *Queen Elizabeth* into Charing Cross Pier and when no one obeyed the quayside cops megaphoned orders to clear the boat, fifty Special Police officers stormed the gang-plank. They dispersed the party with a sickening display of brutally gratuitous violence and two blue meat-wagons were soon filled with assorted members of The Pistols' camp, among them Malcolm McLaren.

The unprecedented police persecution of The Sex Pistols inspired other patriots into Pistol-bashing action throughout June 1977. Johnny Rotten was razored in a Highbury car-park after being recognised in the bar of an adjacent hotel and at Dingwall's Dancehall one week later the boy who had asserted on his very first record that he wanted to destroy the passer-by, was thrown to the ground, hit with a glass and had his chiv-scars re-opened while the club's gawping clientele looked on. As Paul Cook and his girlfriend emerged one night from Shepherd's Bush tube station on the way to his mum's house, he was ambushed by six men who split his head open with iron bars and left him bleeding in the gutter from a would needing fifteen stitches. Four Pistol aides currently sported slashed arms, savaged faces, one broken nose and one broken leg between them.

Bearing in mind McLaren's Machiavellian irresponsibility in matters concerning manipulation of the media, especially his espousal of vicarious violence, the press could hardly be blamed for shrugging off the attacks as merely more gory gimmicks. The papers wanted concrete proof, they wanted photographic evidence, they wanted to see the scars.

The Sex Pistols were amazed that anyone could credit them with such calculated deceit; it seemed just as ridiculous as not being able to walk the streets without a professional bodyguard. The Pistols had always sworn that success would not bar them from tube train, bus-stop, public-bar street-level, as it had the Sixties idols whisked off into mink-lined, bullet-proof cocaine cocoons. With smug cynicism the entire music business/bitter general public had clung to their one comfort – that growing wealth and passing time would mellow and house-train The Sex Pistols into the inviolate isolation of scandal-tabloid adulterers, just like the untamed youth of the previous generation.

But The Pistols didn't closet themselves away from the common man out of choice; they did it because they were in danger of losing their lives. Rotten's car-park assailants hadn't wanted to beat *him* to a pulp so much as carve up The Face Of Punk so thoroughly that he/it would be disfigured for life. Malcolm McLaren's facile "Anarchy as self-rule" mouthings were paying regular visits to the local casualty ward; cops, vigilantes and other thugs were practising what Malcolm preached, and it wasn't society toppling on the precipice of annihilation – it was McLaren and his lads.

As the commercial possibilities of punk rock dawned on every salesman in the land, The Sex Pistols released "Pretty Vacant", their first single not to be banned. Aware of the killing to be made hawking pre-packed teen rebellion, Virgin tempted The Pistols out of twilight-zone paranoia to mime a promotional film-clip of their number seven hit for *Top Of The Pops*, 14 July.

But despite the prime-time The Pistols were given to plug their product, "Pretty Vacant" kept a respectful distance from the supreme niche, and with Matlock's melodies now employed elsewhere, the band's last chance of a number one record was gone forever.

Sensing a blind alley, McLaren began to hold fumbling discussions re A Sex Pistols Starring Vehicle with ketchup-on-pubic-hair film director Russ Meyer. Just back from a Scandinavian tour, the band recorded their debut album between playing a handful of unannounced gigs in small clubs around the UK. Ensconced with Meyer in London and LA, McLaren was too wrapped up in his celluloid aspirations to bother with the tour or the album – playing Nero while The Sex Pistols were burning up with internal friction.

Openly contemptuous of McLaren's 35 millimetre conspiracy, Rotten was sick to the back of his decaying molars with the other Pistols' torpid compliance, and most of all with Meyer himself – Rotten recognising himself as the direct antithesis to someone he considered the archetype fat, rich, patronising, pig-headed American capitalist spewed up by the Sixties permissive-product

Alternative stampede. With McLaren neglecting his duties on the home front and becoming more than ever the band's "manager" in name only, he welcomed the increasingly abrasive relationship between The Pistols themselves. He claimed that the bickering "kept them on their toes" while keeping them too occupied to challenge his jeopardised authority.

The root of all the band's evil was American dancer Nancy Spungen, girlfriend of Sid Vicious, who persuaded the bassist that Rotten's wise decision not to go out without his entourage and bodyguard was nothing more than acute, unjustified paranoia.

If anyone over-estimated their own importance it was Vicious, who caused resentment amongst The Pistols by spending more time trying to become a Rock Dream than learning to play his instrument. Over-compensating for the fact that he could never attract the attention focussed on a lead singer with the distinctive household horror face of Rotten, Vicious sought desperately to become the media's anti-darling by taking Rotten's patented trade-marks to even further extremes. He slashed his body with broken bottles whereas Rotten had stubbed cigarettes out on his arms, attacked antagonists with a rusty bike-chain whereas Rotten was content to dish out verbal lashings, and injected heroin instead of snorting amphetamine.

When Spungen had introduced Vicious to the full-time occupa-tion of wondering where the next fix was coming from, The Pistols camp almost succeeded where the Home Office had failed in deporting her back to the States (the Yankee had been spared on this occasion when Vicious appeared in court claiming he intended to take her for his blushing bride) when they tried to tempt her into an airport-bound car while Sid was in the dentist's chair.

The fleet-footed dancer escaped an Atlantic crossing after infor-ming her kidnappers that if Sid discovered his sweetheart was strapped to an air-borne Jumbo, their facial features would be rearranged with some impromptu plastic surgery courtesy Sid's bike-chain.

On 15 October The Sex Pistols released "Holidays In The Sun", their first plagiarism (of The Jam's "In The City") to date, and the long-awaited unveiling of Sid's songwriting talents. Despite assorted radio bans the record failed to make the Top Five; it also showed that when The Sex Pistols changed bassists they had lost their dance-floor credibility and not their ideological weakness.

On 4 November, the overdue album "Never Mind The Bollocks, Here's The Sex Pistols" was released on an unsuspecting world, which had never dreamed that the nadir of Pistols singles would be the veritable nirvana of Sid's composing capabilities. The Vicious royalty cheques came from "Holidays In The Sun", "Bodies" and

"EMI" – trite, lethargic exercises in negative repetition, sad, vacuous and lame. Almost a greatest hits compilation with no less than a third of the album (weigh it) taken up by the band's four singles; "Liar" and "New York" were ineffectual flicks of the wrist almost as weak as the Vicious efforts; while "Seventeen", "Problems", "No Feelings" and "Submission" were gems from the vault and no excuse.

As Smiths, Boots and Woolworths banned the album, the IBA banned all advertisements for the product and an Edinburgh branch of Virgin Record Shops received several threatening phone calls before being pelted with squelchy foodstuffs for displaying their "Bollocks", bearded Virgin chief Dicky Branson was prosecuted and fined under the 1916 VD Act.

The National Front newspaper *Bulldog* proclaimed Johnny Rotten "no better than a white nigger" and Rotten showed his feelings towards the loathsome slugs when he enrolled in the newly-formed Anti-Nazi League.

Towards the end of the year, Malcolm McLaren kissed Hollywood (and Russ Meyer) goodbye forever when his celluloid visions took a one-way trip to the knacker's yard and the tiresome home-movie was finally forgotten.

As the band prepared to embark upon a world tour, "Belsen Was A Gas", a song Sid Vicious had composed for a previous band, was introduced into their set. After being the only member of the band to turn up for a rehearsal, Vicious tried to end it all by jumping from a hotel's third-storey window but was thwarted by the shear brute strength of Nancy Spungen when she grabbed his belt and plucked him out of the cold night air.

Sid celebrated his new lease of life by banging Nancy's head against the wall until her screams brought the police, who carted the courting couple off to the cells together with various substances for analysis.

The State Department's decision to refuse The Pistols American visas because of speed and violence convictions was reversed after the intervention of an influential peanut-mogul, and the band flew in to commence their nineteen-gig US tour in Atlanta, Georgia, at the beginning of 1978 under the surveillance of Vice Squad officers anticipating another Pearl Harbour.

Heading for San Francisco, the tour wound its ragged way through the Deep South with the Bible-belt audiences striving to act punky for the benefit of the subdued Pistols. Memphis saw 300 peevish ticket holders smash glass doors when they couldn't get in, while on stage Vicious performed his predictable party-trick of indulging in a little self-mutilation with a broken bottle. At Randy's Rodeo in Texas the pogoing rednecks were made to lay down their arms as they entered the auditorium, and when Sid teased them "All you cowboys are faggots!", bombarded the stage with beer cans and drove the bassist to pummel a front-row heckler's head with his guitar. In San Francisco two West Coast would-be punkettes tried to win Sid's heart by punching him full in the face and leaving him with a severely bloodied nose.

When Rotten refused to have any part in McLaren's projected publicity stunt of flying the band down to Rio de Janeiro for a set featuring penniless fugitive Ronald Biggs reading poetry, McLaren accused Rotten of not living up to his name, of not writing any new songs because he wasn't getting along with Steve Jones, and said it was pointless to continue if Rotten refused to go along with ideas like the Rio trip.

The band who had breathed life into the Seventies went their separate ways – Jones and Cook, ever obedient, flying down to Rio for a holiday in the sun with the middle-aged jail-bird Biggs; Vicious once again making the tabloids with yet another conveniently unsuccessful suicide bid, over-dosing on Valium and alcohol in mid-flight from San Francisco to New York; Rotten flying alone to New York, and staying with *New Musical Express* photographer Joe Stevens for a week before returning to London.

So The Sex Pistols avoided becoming The Rolling Stones of the Eighties with the most constructive move they had made since their formation – disintegration. "Malcolm was setting me up to be another Rod Stewart and when I kicked back he didn't like it. I won't work again with any of them and that's no great pity", concluded Johnny Rotten, always as indispensable to The Sex Pistols *per se* as Glen Matlock had been to their melodies.

"Steve can go off and be Peter Frampton; Sid can go off and kill himself and nobody will care; Paul can go back to being an electrician; and Malcolm will always be a Wally."

# ROXY

When The Sex Pistols intuitively kicked back as the audience aimed bottles at their heads during their very first gig, the number of live venues created by the Pub Rock stalwarts began to dwindle; boarding their windows, battering their hatches, locking their door and throwing away the key every time a safety-pin was sighted on the horizon.

Andy Czezowski, a former GLC rent collector and laboratory technician, cut up clothes for Malcolm McLaren and lied that he had master-minded *Sex* while McLaren managed The New York Dolls stateside. Generally known as "a well-meaning loser", Czezowski lived up to his reputation when in February 1976 he became manager of gormless London punk band The Damned – soon losing the post when he failed to find them anywhere to play, except a warehouse.

Czezowski's ex-boss, and owner of King's Road shop *Acme Attractions* (now *Boy*), had erected a punk band called Chelsea around his young chum Gene October, former full-frontal flesh fodder for homosexual skin-rags. Bearing no malice even after his back-up boys kicked him out and asked Czezowski to manage them as Generation X, gay-bar *habitué* Gene informed Andy of a WC2 dive called The Roxy, which around 1974 had done a roaring trade as Chaguarama's Club.

A week before Christmas 1976, Czezowski arranged a trial run of weekly punk gigs, those featuring Generation X and The Heart-breakers paying their way by word of mouth. Czezowski was fired with sufficient enthusiasm to lease the club full-time as the UK's first exclusively punk rock venue, opening 1 January 1977 with The Clash.

Unleashed, the movement's troops flocked to the subterranean Soho oven with the passion of persecuted religious dissidents – posing at the bar with obsessive dedication, pogoing like epileptic dervishes to the onstage acts pumping out endless three-chord wastelands. In the beginning, a Roxy gig would always boast more stars at the upstairs bar than both the stage and the tatty, enthusiastic audience put together.

Upstairs, a tiny space of personal territory was the first priority; outbreaks of violence were infinite but quickly checked by nothing more than the confinement of the crowd – only when a handful of human dregs lingered, kicking at the lager can scrap-heap, did the workshy bouncers make their presence felt.

When The Roxy played host to a status band, the Great British

Queue of working punters would stretch halfway round the block while the coveted faces sauntered straight in, referred to the guest-list and conceived a battle-plan to get to the bar. Around this minute, extortionate shrine clustered professional malchicks, their egos as delicate as painted eggshells, languidly engaged in conversation while their restless eyes cast around relentlessly for someone still higher on the status ladder of punkdom.

They were the type of people who hung out till closing time for fear of what might be said about them if they left. With all the *joie de vivre* of those attending their own funerals, they would flounce desperately back and forth before the record company executives, the pockets of whose Street Chic jackets burst with the contracts suddenly begging for the signature of any punk sensation that was still warm.

As opposed to the alluringly lurid press hand-outs featuring fishnet stockings, spiked heels and bondage, these kiddies looked nothing if not nastily neuter in the cold, clammy flesh beneath their revulsion-conscious efforts. Their clothes were elaborately contrived to make the wearer appear as terrifyingly repugnant as possible, alluding to anything that would induce immediate outrage in the eye of the beholder – sore points like sado-masochism, fascism and gender confusion. Hair shorn close to the skull and dyed any colour so long as it didn't look *natural*, spiked up with Vaseline; noses, ears, cheeks, lips and other extremities pierced with a plethora of safety-pins, chains and dangling insignia; ripped and torn jumble sale shirts, strangled with a thin tie and mutilated with a predictable graffiti of song titles, perversions or Social Observations; black leather wristbands and dog-collars studded with silver spikes, sometimes with leashes attached; trouser legs tied together; zips, buckles and various scrap metal embellishing leather, vinyl, rubberwear and plastic bin-liners.

And on top, like just another personalised aberration – A Face, black or red glossy man-hole mouth, set in a face of death pallor artifice below eyes of black and white, Frankenstein and Vampirella *maquillage*.

Their blood, however, flowed not from a perforated neck but from a speed-scorched sinus. For the first time since the Renaissance, amphetamine was being used as a cosmetic in much the same way as certain fourteenth century girls ate the fatal stimulant Belladonna, to make the pupils dilate and give their eyes the fashionable appearance of huge black saucers.

The look of amphetamine psychosis became desirable when the mass of new wave disciples fell in love with their mirror-image innovators The Sex Pistols (amphetamine cognoscenti long before their early celebration of the drug in "Seventeen"), making it necessary for the less adventurous at least to *simulate* the appearance of sulphate-snorters; cold, piercing stares, exaggerated black and white doe-eyes, blanched make-up, rapid speech and an aura of a capacity for ultra-violent aggression.

The Roxy's chaste ambience – so striking that the uninformed onlooker would think that the house lager had been spiked with bromide – was emphasised by the number of punk patrons running with a pack containing no members of the opposite sex, and the inclination of those on a night out with the boys to hang out without inhibition in the girls room. Here, speeding clientele gazed into the mirrors hypnotised by their own wall-to-wall reflections, induced by the self-obsessive properties of the pharmaceutical which also gave sufficient energy to encourage the deluge of fanzines that sprang up in the wake of Mark P's *Sniffin' Glue*.

Hawked by their authors at the top of The Roxy stairs – leading down to the basement's eardrum-shredding drone – fanzines were homemade alternative press which would have been impossible among the previous generation of contented cannabis consumers; stapled pages of photo-copied reviews, gossip, gig guides and unrelieved fawning over any punky feet that had graced a stage.

The fanzine format was first tried and tested in the late summer of 1976 when unemployed Mark Perry of Deptford produced *Sniffin' Glue 1*. The William Rees-Mogg of Xeroxed adulation, Mark P saw a new band every night and was therefore justifiably discerning when assessing the merits of individual bands and putting his influential opinions down on paper. He constantly baited his readers out of their satiated rebellion – and for this reason despised The Roxy – and relentlessly bullied *Sniffin' Glue* subscribers to start their own fanzines. Pied-Piper P's success at producing a paper unhampered by corporate structure, cash and censorship led a multitude of irretrievably anonymous kids to duplicate issues of their very own dog-eared dogma – mostly sycophantic punk pap, with a few notable exceptions like Lucy Toothpaste's *Jolt*, Sandra Short's *Hangin' Around* and Randy Bollocker's *These Things*.

At this time the fanzine writers were working-class kids, often known by simply their first names to avoid harassment from Department of Employment officials when paying their weekly visit to the signing-on box, the true spirit of what was then labelled "Dole Queue Rock".

Not so the middle-class punks with parents affluent enough to purchase musical equipment for their offspring. In the basement, the Roxy music itself was mostly dire, few of the neophytes possessing the imaginative flair of the innovators, but the club was home, a real riot of your own and when someone like The Buzzcocks or X-Ray Spex played the atmosphere would be more electric than anything you'd ever experienced in your life. The Roxy would catch fire and chaos would reign.

But as the biggest and best punk bands were signing to major labels and deserting The Roxy for prestigious, profitable, plush-seated concert halls, the album purporting to be an authentic document of the club's halcyon days was recorded on four bad nights at the beginning of April. A con in crusade's clothing, "The Roxy, London WC2" was a perfect compilation for a generation that doesn't dance, released on the first label to fire The Sex Pistols – EMI.

*That* band's cussing may have caused EMI to flush in anger, but the record company managed to cover their sheltered ears to the excerpts of ethnic expletives gilding The Roxy album, as it became the first live recording to make the Top Twenty album charts since the Bangla Desh Benefit Concert. This high placing may not have been unconnected with EMI's marketing technique of offering record shops a name-check on the double-page Roxy album advertisements only if they promised to take at least 25 copies of the record.

The product itself was a rush-job managing to omit almost all of the finest bands who had played The Roxy, instead gathering together an interminable tinny drone, unlistenable mindless muzak which sounded as if it had been recorded in a rusty baked bean can.

Nevertheless, by spring 1977 the influx of weekend punks, freak-spotting, camera-toting tourists and the buck-hungry lust of record company exploitrepreneurs all using The Roxy to scramble aboard a bandwagon that was already losing its wheels, made Andy Czezowski finally admit: "The Roxy is finished with the hardcore new wave kids."

The Roxy was also finished with Czezowski. After neglecting to pay the £25,000 annual rent, he was physically ejected by the club's owner Rene Albert one Saturday night in mid-April with orders never to return.

Without Czezowski's empathy, The Roxy degenerated into a cheapskate burger joint with a compulsory plate-of-chips purchase before you could sit down. An attempt by the GLC to close the Roxy on grounds of raucous punk behavior was forgotten after the club lost its stranglehold as number one punk venue, the kids forsaking the anachronism for dimly-lit pastures new.

Today The Roxy stands as a headstone to former glory where the punks had once gone to be bored for posterity.

# CONVOY

Once the bandwagon had been given wheels by the sudden desire of every record company to possess a punk band, every band was suddenly Punk.

The mass of raw repressed energy, mutated into pockets of feverish action by the example of The Sex Pistols, was never a genuine *movement* – just a collection of non-starter rat-racers who didn't lack the greed for fame and fortune so patently obvious in the idols they professed to despise, just the Old Guard's technical proficiency. The advent of punk required not virtuosity of music, but of attitude – the new wave's only revolutionary reform was that now *anyone* could become a tax-exile.

As punk rock became a potential product-shifter, bands began to brush up their own unique selling-points in the hope of tempting the best and biggest label in town. By the spring of 1977, there were four established Pretenders to The Sex Pistols' inviolate throne – The Damned, The Jam, The Clash and The Stranglers. Their names never became household-words synonymous with "Punk Rock", but all four consoled themselves with hooking a meal-ticket from a major label.

First on the block to ape the guiding light Pistols, and evolve their own distinct individual image were The Damned. A shoddy mob of burlesque queens and reformed hippies intent on riding the crest of the new wave, The Damned were formed in the summer of 1976 and comprised Brian James, ex-London SS on guitar, ex-grave-digger Dave "Letts" Vanian on vocals, and a previously unemployed rhythm section of Rat "Chris Miller" Scabies on drums with Captain "Ray Burns" Sensible on bass. Signed that August by Stiff Records after playing at the French Mont de Marsan festival – the first punk event ever – The Damned compensated for their monumental lack of lyrical imagination and inability to write melodically memorable music with a complete repertoire cranked out at a hopefully indecipherable speed, and a visual decoy consisting of camp-caped Vanian in cut-price Count Dracula fancy-dress and make-up, plus a village-idiot Sensible imitating a defective Dalek decked out in ballerina's tutu or white nurse's uniform.

Characteristically, The Damned initiated the punk custom of "gobbing" in the course of their artless aspirations to Rotten's audience-provocation. On day two of The 100 Club's Punk Festival of September 1976, one of the numerous glasses aimed at The Damned by an audience the band had deliberately set out to antagonise into front-page lynch-mob vengeance, splintered and ricocheted off a pillar – blinding the eighteen-year-old girl.

The tragedy created obscenely less public outrage and subsequent backlash than either The Sex Pistols swearing on live TV, or their anti-monarchy statement "God Save The Queen". But the immediate punk ban activated by the sole small venues open, combined with The Damned's tame and mercenary mindlessness, made them the most distrusted figures on the punk scene – their quisling reputation confirmed when they were kicked off The Sex Pistols "Anarchy" tour after just one gig, for asserting that they were still prepared to play even if The Sex Pistols were censored.

The Damned were established as the punk band that would do everything first *and* worst; first punk single "New Rose" failing to make the Top Twenty in November 1976, first punk album "Damned, Damned, Damned" failing to make the Top Twenty album chart in February 1977, first punk band to tout for the teeny-bopper-market when they promoted their second flop single "Neat, Neat, Neat" on pop programme *Supersonic*, and the first punk band to go down like a dead weight in the USA when they bombed at New York City's prestigious CBGB club in April 1977.

After a summer spent suffering from the side-effects of Stiff Records flexing their media-manipulative muscles, the drowning Damned clutched at Lu, a parrot-faced second guitarist who made his undistinguished debut with The Damned at the 1977 Mont de Marsan Festival. Here, the desperate Captain Sensible's fumbling publicity stunt of strolling onstage during the headlining Clash set to break open a selection of stink-bombs resulted in the Captain being thrown high into the air, and eventually coming to land with a leg either side of a spiked iron fence. Regaining consciousness, the Captain found himself lying on a stretcher being loaded into an ambulance, and screamed in a voice several octaves higher than usual before fleeing the stretcher to seek refuge on top of a parked van, hotly pursued by both the stretcher-bearers and the van's owner.

Back in England, The Damned's impotent American exploits became public knowledge and the band were soon generally recognised as being as pathetic as they looked. Scabies had boasted of his carnal conquest of Runaway Joan Jett to the press and to London rock society at large, forced to retract his fantasies when Joan wrote an indignant letter of denial to the *New Musical Express*; both Scabies and Sensible had scrounged drinks with anecdotes of their sexual assault upon a New York groupie with a Fender Bass.

The Damned were Untouchables, scorned by the punks they had disowned and snubbed by the pop-kids they had sought to embrace. In October 1977 Rat Scabies failed in a suicide bid, but managed to quit the band, before failing an audition for the post of drummer with Johnny Thunders' Heartbreakers. Making the first accurate judgement of his life, Scabies described The Damned's recently released album "Music For Pleasure" as an unsuccessful attempt to mimic The Rolling Stones' acid-mush "Satanic Majesties".

Produced by Pink Floyd producer Nick Mason and featuring jazz saxophonist Lol "Chrome Dome" Coxhill, the album wallowed from beginning to end in whining self-pity as The Damned directed their trite tirades at their numerous adversaries, only succeeding in making themselves appear more ineffectual than ever.

The Damned's record-time descent to the very depths of the music industry continued into the last two months of 1977, when the fans stayed away in droves from the band's minutely attended UK tour, with replacement John Moss on drums and American band The Dead Boys on support.

In the first month of 1978 The Damned's manager Dave Robinson quit the sinking ship, taking his Stiff recording contract with him.

Trail-blazers to the bitter end, The Damned have become the first lepers of punk. In February 1978 they were eaten away forever.

Strong contenders for the title are The Jam. Despite being two hit singles and a recording contract up, The Jam are the only Fab Four band to be hampered by many of the pitfalls that destroyed The Damned.

Both bands are the brainchild of lower-middle-class Tories, abhorred by all self-respecting punks for disassociating themselves from a movement which they had no qualms about cashing in on. Safely sheltered under the fashionable punk banner, their debut albums achieved chart success – out on a free-enterprising limb both second albums were commercially and artistically miserable failures. After becoming hot properties by virtue of their punk following, both bands deserted their fans for a pot-shot at the hypermarkets of teeny-telly and Hip Easy Rebellion America – but finding Carter country apathetic, puppy-love fickle, and the new wave suddenly hostile, they could never go home again.

Formed in Woking, Surrey, in 1972 when 14-year-old guitarist Paul Weller got together with bassist Bruce Foxton and drummer Rick Buckler, both 17, to jam during school lunch-breaks, the band was named by the boys in a moment of inspiration. After two years of Surrey youth-club obscurity, Paul Weller – The Jam's youngest and most intelligent member and also their manager's son – transferred schoolboy loyalties from The Beatles to The Who after hearing "My Generation". By the time The Jam began playing London at the end of 1976, their instant-image was crystallised as contemporary Shepherd's Bush Mod.

Dressed in black and white spats, black ties and white shirts set off by three-buttoned jackets and flared mohair strides (a paradox, but how were non-Mod audiences to know?), The Jam tore through a re-vamped repertoire that had gradually replaced Mod museum-pieces with Weller's own.

Their sound was a time-warped souvenir sure to win favour within the reactionary mass of the music industry, Weller playing a profusion of critic-charming chopped Townshend chords and archaic scratched R & B lead rhythm guitar. Sidekicks Foxton and Buckler sounded equally born-too-late.

The Jam's all-important membership-card meal-ticket into the new wave were Weller's lyrics; anxious to be included amongst the new crusaders against rock stagnation yet afraid to risk an unpopular political stance, The Jam fell back on that evergreen rock and roll cop-out the Generation Gap. Their youth-unity polemics urged young people to "stick together" and celebrate "the young idea" with songs like "Art School" and "Time For Truth" as if the common enemy was defined by nothing more than the passing of time.

Weller's masquerade as a sensitive soul outraged into rebellion had attracted both EMI and Polydor by the start of 1977 – the former shying off once bitten by The Sex Pistols thus leaving the field clear for Polydor (left at the altar by both The Damned and The Clash) to sign their hard-won "punk band" The Jam. But those who sign are blind – looking through the rose-tinted glasses of invest-ment, Polydor failed to register that The Jam's most controversial gesture to date had been to burn a copy of *Sniffin' Glue* onstage at the Marquee after the fanzine had described them as "laid-back".

Top Twenty placings in spring for their "In The City" single and album earned The Jam second billing on The Clash's first UK tour. Piqued by their paucity of sound-checks, the second fiddles soon pulled out to prepare for their own headlining summer tour; it culminated in a disastrous climax at the box-office-bankroll Ham-mersmith "Air Hanger" Odeon, where The Jam turned the censored-sound-check tables on *their* support act The Boys, forcing them to leave the stage after just two numbers.

The Jam further tarnished their Brave New Order image when at the last minute they pulled out of the August Mont de Marsan Punk Festival rather than face an audience intoxicated by old-timers Dr Feelgood. Two months later they got to play three Stateside gigs, and wished they hadn't.

In November The Jam's second album "This Is The Modern World" found the band overstretched, tuneless and bitter, having wet-dreams of tower-blocks in Woking. They had finally abandoned dance tunes and mohair for severely constipated social comment;

the romantic interest of their boy-girl interludes ultimately exposed as nothing but serenades beneath Margaret Thatcher's balcony.

Untamed, Paul Weller demanded – "What better way to get a message across than through a memorable tune that you can whistle?"

No better way, Paul – why don't you have a bash?

Weller is the Barry McGuire of Punk.

The Clash, on the other hand, are the MC5 of the new wave; the credibility-hustling manager, the six-figure recording contract, the revolution for fun and profit. They were formed in 1976 from unsatisfactory drummer Terry Chimes – fired and re-hired constantly throughout 1976 and early 1977 – junkie guitarist Keith Levine plus upwardly-mobile art students Mick Jones on guitar and vocals and Paul Simenon on bass.

While taking a constitutional down the Portobello Road, Jones, Simenon and Sex Pistol Glen Matlock ran into diminutive diplomat's son John Mellor, who they recognised as Joe Strummer of pub-rockers The 101-ers. They informed Strummer that he was great though his band were garbage, and highly impressed with Jones and Simenon's clothes, Joe joined The Clash after talks with their manager Bernie Rhodes.

Keith Levine was soon too involved with heroin to devote any time to playing guitar, and quit The Clash leaving behind him only one song "What's My Name" and his candid appearances in Bernie's home movies.

"I've got some great shots of Keith fixing up in the toilet", Bernie once enthused.

Astute readers will remember Bernie as Malcolm McLaren's chauffeur in chapter two. Previously a used-car salesman, Bernie had first infiltrated the *demi-monde* as Vivienne Westwood's lying printer – claiming to have conceived *all* the *Sex* T-shirts when he has in fact created only the *You're Going To Wake Up One Morning And Discover Which Side Of The Bed You're On* mode.

Ecstatic that The Clash now boasted a bit of posh who had previously been in a band named after Orwell's *1984* torture-chamber and formed by Chilean refugee Alvaro, Rhodes set about using Strummer, Jones and Simenon (the numerous drummers used by the band have always been anonymous nonentities) as three blank T-shirts on which to superimpose his own self-conscious political posturing, and as showroom dummies for his custom-made urban battle-fatigues inspired by a picture-book of soldiers' uniforms through the ages, at this moment in time not returned to Camden Library.

All that remained was for Joe Strummer to be taught to walk by a genuine working-class boy – Clash camp-follower Robin Banks –

before Bernie sent them out on the bottom of the "Anarchy" bill as a glib alternative to the furious vacancy of The Sex Pistols.

By March 1977, record companies great and small were longing for their very own punk band. Polydor were giving The Clash full use of their studios and the band were on the verge of signing until sought out by fat-cats CBS and swept off to Soho Square with a £100,000 contract – worthy stable-mates for Andy Williams and Abba.

In April The Clash released their debut album, and one week later it had reached number twelve in the album chart. The front cover captured them as three pious mannequins caught with their legs open while the back of the sleeve flaunted a massed-police charge on black youths under the Westway flyover at the 1976 Notting Hill Carnival.

They were the first band to use social disorder as a marketing technique to shift product – "I have gobbed in the eye of the whirlwind – please buy my record." Deceptively, The Clash were the only punk band other than The Pistols whose music didn't sound like a rehashed resurrection re-tread of some Sixties anachronism. Lyrically, as befitted someone who had joined The Clash merely because he loved the way Jones and Simenon looked, Strummer's hammy histrionic anger dabbled in casual destruction as a stage-prop.

"Who needs the Parliament, sitting making laws all day? . . . Can't make no noise! . . . Hate and war, the only things we got today! . . . I hate Englishmen just as bad as wops! . . . The truth is only known by guttersnipes! . . . Big businessman don't like you, don't like the things you do! . . . I don't wanna go fighting in the tropical heat! . . . I just wanna stay in the garage all night!"

When po-faced Joe could be tempted away from the micro-phone, Mick Jones chanted stray battle-cries like a harassed housewife while throughout the record The Clash axe-picking was redolent of a bunch of buskers playing Spanish guitars in an expense-account trattoria.

The band had been manufactured by the lying printer of *Sex* Bernie Rhodes (in direct competition to Mal's Pistols), but The Clash had worked so hard at maintaining an impressive visual that they had neglected content for style, reduced to inventing problems that didn't exist as satisfactory lapel-badges. Symptomatic of The Clash as frustrated window-dressers were – Bernie's CLASH number plate; Strummer's de-elocution lessons; a snooker game set up for the benefit of a "realistic" interview – contrived spontaneity; politics as "abstract theatre" (Bernie's phrase) in their perennial stage back-drop of the Notting Hill riots, until they visited Belfast for a photo-session; Strummer ringing up the *New Musical*

*Express* complaining that the pictures printed "weren't flattering".

After several White Rhetoric tours around Britain, The Clash attended the plush-lush CBS Convention and sangalongwith Artie Garfunkel to The Beached Boys. They continued to bellow their battlecries, stealing hotel linen and grabbing themselves a *Sunday Times* spread. At their early 1977 Rainbow apex their daring reached new depths when Joe incited those nearest the stage to uproot their seats. The Army was not called in. The establishment never so much as trembled in its well-heeled shoes.

In July Birmingham's councillors vetoed the Clash gig planned for Digbeth Rag Market during a fit of punk-purging, but the band issued a communique stating that they intended to play the gig despite official censorship. Bernie, who had been looking at too many soldier picture-books, dreamed of bringing out the heavy artillery to join the Clash convoy up the M1.

"Driving two tanks right up to the gates of the market!" Rhodes twittered.

"Imagine that! I can just see Paul in an armoured car . . . but even if you hire them you can't get a licence to drive them on the motorway."

Would *you* buy a used riot from this man?

The rambling minstrels arrived in the vicinity of the Rag Market at seven in the rain. Fearing for their spikey hairstyles, Jones, Simenon and their latest drummer Nicky Headon squirmed further into the snug security of their American press officer's car, leaving Strummer to make his pilgrimage to the closed market gates of red steel alone.

There some thirty kids, soaked to the skin, had gathered, ignoring the repeated police warnings to stay away broadcast on the radio. After talking briefly to them, Strummer was gently moved on by two amiable cops and the entire Clash convoy retired to a nearby pub, where Headon expressed his disapproval of all authority by firing peas at innocent drinkers while Simenon favoured a pink plastic water pistol as a means of inciting teen rebellion.

After pulling off several manoeuvres, Bernie Rhodes managed to transform the storming of Digbeth Rag Market into a gig at the chrome and plastic chicken-in-a-basket discotheque, Barbarella's.

Rhodes thought the whole day was "abstract theatre", but everyone else thought it was pathetic.

Unlike MC5 manager John Sinclair, Bernie Rhodes didn't go to jail – instead he clung like a leech. Mick Jones *almost* joined Glen Matlock's Rich Kids because Rhodes refused to give him a living wage, but the closest The Clash came to biting the hand that formed them was after Bernie left the room in the early days of the Capital Radio recording session – when Strummer, Jones and Simenon jumped up and down upon his leather jacket after flinging it to the floor.

In spring 1978, The Clash are in the same position as they were this time last year; touring the UK cranking out the same old chestnuts and inspiring just enough audience reaction to get tin cans thrown at the stage, releasing failure singles like the abysmal "Clash City Rockers", and locking themselves in the studio to record an album, when Strummer isn't confined to a hospital bed with hepatitis.

Bernie's favourite song is "The Monkees Theme".

"Here we come/Walking down the street/We get the funniest looks from/Everyone we meet."

"This next bit is my favourite," beams balding Bernie.

"We're the young generation/And we got something to say/Hey hey we're The Monkees!"

The Clash are single-dimension art scholars – they're too busy singing to put anybody down.

Whereas The Stranglers are too preoccupied with their own stunted sexuality to offer any contribution to tangible political issues other than pathetically limp lip-service.

They got together in early 1974 as The Guildford Stranglers, with mid-twenties gangling graduate Hugh Cornwell on guitar, ex-Nazi Jean Burnel on the biggest bass bread could buy, fat forties Phyllosan Generation ex-jazz drummer and ice-cream man Jet Black and Dave Greenfield on keyboards and moustache, who used to wear his shoulder-length hair in a pony-tail – until punk happened, forcing David to drop the bow.

The only thing that could be forwarded in The Stranglers' favour was that prior to punk they were on the road for eighteen months playing regularly at places most bands didn't know existed. Unlike the younger punkies who came up out of nowhere immediately to score a recording contract, The Stranglers were plodders. They were finally awarded a United Artists recording deal not for ability but for effort.

But in this case, their prep paid off; their first album "Rattus Norvegicus IV" sold 30,000 copies in its first two weeks, eventually notching up a silver disc for sales of £150,000. United Artists counted units and washed their hands of the blood.

Basically, The Stranglers were the colonising influence of the new wave . . . Mary Whitehouse's pristine psyche stamped onto The Doors' best heavy psychedelic riffs. Erected on the tried-and-true foundations of the Manly Virtues i.e. misogyny, latent homosexuality and heavy physical exercise, preferably in the communal shower, "Rattus Norvegicus IV" caught them in the raw.

Laying such a stress on the Brotherhood of Man, The Stranglers appealed equally to Heavy Metal fans in denim and long hair, safety-pin punky fledglings, sporting crews of team-game enthusiasts plus the mass of Pop Kids who were alienated by the more intelligent punk bands (The Stranglers were the only new wave band with degrees, but they were thick as shit).

Despite holding new wave meal-tickets, The Stranglers had no interest in any form of progress whatsoever, and were in every way an old-fashioned almost medieval band of manky minstrels, hung up on plagues of disease-carrying rats circa 1665, doomy Gothic organ-grinding and the warped, blinkered middle-class Surrealist Ethic (probably picked up on campus) that believes anything is permissible as long as it's done in the name of the inviolate godhead Art. Jean Burnel, an admirer of the Kray brothers and karate who believes that male children should be raised as "warriors", had a successful fit of the vapours when called up for the French army, and his dilettante's love of violence-voyeurism induced karma comeback when The Stranglers visited Canterbury and Burnel's hand was bitten by an irate young Smokie fan from a local council estate.

"I hate people like you", the kid sneered at Burnel.

Studying *Hereward The Wake* for his history degree exam had never been like this! Inevitably, after cramming for so long, Burnel considered himself to be the brains behind any operation, and therefore employed a working-class private army who called themselves The Finchley Boys to handle "warrior" duties.

Incidentally, The Stranglers' second album contained a tribute to one "Dagenham Dave", a former Number One Fan who committed suicide when his place in The Stranglers' affections was usurped by the Finchley Buds.

Their second album "No More Heroes" was intended as an affirmation of their "political" stance, but it only succeeded in emphasising the totally vacuous nature of their portentous polemics. Though they claim to be Trotskyists, Leon Trotsky would have abhorred their hysterical sexism.

In fact, according to Cornwell, The Stranglers have not once voted. The extent of their political sus is best summed up by Hughie himself: "Jo Grimond, to me, really seemed to be pretty okay. But he was freaked out. Grimond has gone to the Shetland Isles and they're going to have a lot of oil."

The Stranglers are such good liberals that they will even bend for the BBC and delete swear words from singles that look like they've got a chance of getting airplay. Consequently, they have been awarded more hit singles than any other "punk" band.

The only thing The Stranglers are anti – is women.

While their contempt for femininity is pushed as merely another facet of their massive masculinity, Wilhelm Reich might analyse it as a pubescent smut/old maid's distaste for the healthy animalism of humanity. A nightmare of reality in which sex, dirt and vermin are interchangeable.

"We're into acid", offers Cornwell.

It shows.

# AMERICANS

No American new wave band likes another – but they all have clean butts and a nasty taste in their mouths.

For a relatively young nation, the USA is remarkably slow when it comes to tapping talent – even though sucking the cents out of every available European culture is the national pastime. Why, even France caught on to punk rock quicker!

I mean, Americans think it's punky to be a junkie!

All American bands bray that "punk" is a label invented by a scared press, but everyone tried to ride in on the new wave. The advent of an art-form where technical ability was not prerequisite inspired the Land Of Axe Heroes no-hopers (over-27 Division) to come crawling out of the woodwork for one last desperate grab at that brass ring.

New York's crass and glossy *Punk* magazine poses as a State-side equivalent of the UK fanzines while sycophantically fawning over the grossest old repented hippy masquerading as a wrinkled punk. As long as they tow the native New Yorker nihilist line, *Punk* continues to print the mangy old mugs of mutton like Ugly Dickhead Manilow and the Dictators, Wayne County and Fester Bangs.

The generation gap protecting the whole catalogue of UK fanzines from the humdrum scum of *Punk* exactly parallels the chasm between the bands of both countries. British new wave music comes from underprivilege and class discrimination – its lyrics are bitter and optimistic. But America is too far gone, and its bands have retreated into selfish fantasies of individual reality.

The American Dream is piled upon the vision of accumulating enough money to permit them to give the problems of the huddled masses a derisive finger. *In $ They Trust* ... in a nation of failed Henry Fords where even health must be bought, you can take the Yankee out of Wall Street but you can't take Wall Street out of the Yankee.

Simply, English punk bands want to be the best – American punk bands want to be the richest.

Manhattan is not an island ·for nothing – outside of Max's and CBGB's, kids still light candles for Kiss and The Bee Gees. But the Rotten Apple itself is plagued with maggots ... hundreds of bands fashionable for a fortnight, their creative genius beginning and ending at coming up with suitably "shocking" and "artistic" names: The Good Rats, Suicide, Day Old Bread, Laughing Dogs, The Mumps, Pretty Poison, Another Pretty Face, The Psychotic Frogs.

Energies exhausted concocting an appropriate handle, these

bands spend more time playing with themselves (and each other) than playing gigs.

But even New York City's favourite sons are disowned in their own country. A handful of American new wave acts may annually pack out British concert halls but in their homeland, lack of interest (the youth of the country all out throwing fire-crackers at Aerosmith and dropping downers) forces Yankee Punkees into the "intimate" atmosphere of tiny clubs.

In the land of the brave and free, punks are an even smaller minority than socialists – though nowhere near as feared, naturally.

Remember – Uncle Sam says "Better crop-head than Red!"

But what can an Artist Type do but sing in a rock and roll band?

Last year's cult kingpin was pouting Thomas Verlaine and his "Lice Queens Of Rock" Television. The name was originally chosen as high satire, though eventually the plot would sicken.

Television was formed by Tom Verlaine (né Miller) and Richard Hell (né Myers), old room-mates from rich-kids' school, when they eloped to New York City in 1973, and made their performing debut a year later, somehow scoring a regular gig at everyone's favourite Bowery slum – CBGB's.

They were so esoteric that they inevitably attracted ex-Roxy Music chrome-dome dilettante Brian Eno, who became a Dada-figure for the band and tried to capture their tortured genes on tape.

However, the band lost something in tape-translation – namely Verlaine's parade of facial grimaces serving to portray the inner torments of French Symbolist as fish-fingered axe-hero. Verlaine subsequently began to slur his words when singing, keeping his cherished lyrics locked in an indecipherable vault and thereby preventing the other poets on his block from plagiarising his precious prose.

Verlaine and sidekick Hell shared a chummy chuckle when they auditioned fellow heroin-enthusiast Dee Dee Ramone and blackballed the blank bassist's entry to the band when it transpired that one could count the number of chords Dee Dee knew on his waxy ear-holes.

But Hell's humour died in his throat when Tom put business before pleasure and gave Hell his cards due to Dicky's "musical incapabilities". With Hell perusing the Situations Vacant columns, Verlaine was left happy as a Surrealist sand-boy, backed by a band as faceless as session men and as functional as wallpaper.

In 1975 Television released a song called "Little Johnny Jewel" on New York's Dork Records – the only known label as snobbish and fey as Telly themselves. The only people who bought it were New Yorkers who believed that they were reincarnations of French homosexual poets.

After literally *buying* the eyesore London Bridge when their hearts had been set on picturesque *Tower* Bridge, and with this decade's British Invasion led by The Sex Pistols looming ominously on the New York skyline, America was determined to grow some culture of her own. In the stampede to secure the signatures of the leading freaks of the latest fad, the American record labels failed to perceive that these new rebels were troubled by wrinkles rather than acne. Understandable, in an Education For Cash country where a 30-year-old could be fresh out of school.

Thus Elektra signed Television at the end of 1976, giving British release to their album "Marquee Moon" at the start of 1977. It was salivated upon by the Sixties debris of a music press still Stateside-struck and anxious for the latest Transatlantic tyrant whose every damp fart could be analysed for the archives – In America *We* Trust!

But for your money, you got four tracks on each side – common "cult" practice. And *these* few gems would have been half the size had not they played host to guitar solos that would outdo Segovia.

Though Hosanna'd as though they'd walked on water rather than strummed on guitars, "Marquee Moon" recalled nothing so much as fledgling Byrds had they aimed for a date with Salvador Dali rather than the Top Ten.

Lyrically, Verlaine came across as an acid-babbling Edward Lear who had worn out a crateful of "Sergeant Pepper's Lonely Hearts Club Band".

"I woke up and it's yesterday ... Life in the hive puckered up my night ... I want a nice little boat made out of ocean ... Chirp chirp the birds, they're giving you the words."

Naturally, such pearls went down a storm when Television toured Britain in summer 1977. Each prematurely-converted audience gawped at Tom-Boy like he was Luke Skywanker from *Star Wars* with a Ph.D in inhumanity – surely the antithesis of "rock and roll"?

In fact, all that can be said in Television's favour is that European Elektra supremo Moira "The Mod" Bellas once had a schoolgirl crush on Verlaine – and that they're good to their British fans in that Television rarely tour these isles.

Their last album, "Adventure", stinks.

Whereas Johnny Thunders' Heartbreakers were forced to exchange geographical location with the bread-head Anglo tax-exiles, when no Stateside record label would touch them with either needle or contract due to their reputation as long-time self-destructive drug fiends.

The Heartbreakers were formed in 1975, immediately after the plane carrying Johnny Thunders and Jerry Nolan away from the debris of The New York Dolls touched down in Son of Sam's City.

With Nolan on drums and Thunders on lead guitar, The Heart-breakers were completed with second guitarist Walter Lure (resembling the balding bastard offspring of a stick insect and a white-washed Harlem Globetrotter) and, on bass, ex-Television pseudo-seer Richard Hell, who – as Tom Verlaine had done to him – commandeered the band's vocals and thus the leadership. Hell's megalomania was abruptly terminated when his backing band informed him that he was no longer a Heartbreaker.

"I didn't want to back up a lead singer", mouthed Thunders. "I'd backed up a lead singer for too long."

Hell's cinema verité nihilism, executed not with stars but with dollar signs in his eyes, was a rich kid's indulgence incompatable with Thunders, Nolan and Lure's drinking-class obsession with "love songs to objects" – ultimately, celebrations of sex object com-modities, in which girls came a sad second to drugs. Too cool to fool, their happily-married brand-new bassist Billy Rath was never-theless sufficiently subordinate to warm the cockles of The Heart-breakers' hearts.

"Ah prefer drugs to women, anyhow."

In summing up the fatal rock and roll death-wish connection, Johnny Thunders killed his chance of being remembered for any-thing as mundane as music – or for getting The Heartbreakers banned from CBGB's, forcing them to flog a dead horse across England on The Sex Pistols Artifice In The UK tour; the presence of Thunders making it a sentimental journey for all those wide-eyed punks weaned on The New York Dolls.

Duped by the dewy-eyed welcome he received from nostalgic proles poised to take over positions of pop-power, Thunders decided that England swings and became a resident until mid-July when the Home Office discovered that The Heartbreakers' work-permits were not in order – kicking them out forthwith. They returned in time for a rude awakening when the fruits of their long-awaited contract with Track Records were released in October.

The album "L.A.M.F." (Like A Mother Fucker) and its single "Chinese Rocks" (first in a picture-sleeved series that would even-tually duplicate the album, flung at the fan to no avail) were miserable and inevitable failures. For the first time in recording history, produc-tion became an end in itself as the sub-aquatic cassette reproduc-tion elbowed aside the product it should have worked for.

And if the listener bothered to scramble beyond the spiteful sludge of sound, the album's content was nothing more than one-dimension smack-obsession. "Music While You Cold Turkey" – the only people able to relate to The Heartbreakers' "love" songs would be other junkies, and even junkies have better things to do with their money.

In fact, their distaste for anything other than their pharmaceutical sweetheart ("Political bullshit", spat Walter Lure when questioned on the extent of their social conscience) led to the infinite ineptitude pervading all aspects of The Heartbreakers' career. It reached an ugly head when Jerry Nolan quit the band and Track Records ditched The Heartbreakers not quite quick enough to recoup their losses. But the label's business instinct had been born too late, and a month later Track shut up shop for good.

Even sniffing around for a new label, Thunders is still boasting that The Heartbreakers are planning to change their name to The Junkies: "To show that we're a no-holds-barred band."

Untamed, Johnny Thunders was last seen onstage at Dingwall's (a night-club for homeless music business flotsam) playing guitar for well-worn R & B plodders Little Bob Story on "Roll Over Beethoven".

This same humble gig would be as manna from heaven to ex-employee of both Thunders and Tom Verlaine – toad-eyed bassist Richard Hell. Until such a time, Hell sits it out in New York City with his band The Voidoids, dreaming of a shot at the casting-couch.

His dreams first fell through in 1975 when Tom Verlaine threw him out of Television. Within two days The Heartbreakers had given him a good home, where he stayed for one year before delusions of grandeur prompted him to scrape together a band of totally unknown musicians who wouldn't insist he became house-trained.

By virtue of the fact that he had once shared stages with Verlaine and Thunders, Hell soon secured an EP deal with New York's *phlegm de la phlegm* Dork Records. "Blank Generation" was released in Britain on Stiff Records at the end of 1976, and a hired cult swooned while across the sea The Voidoids tuned up at mock-Mecca CBGB's for their first ever gig. The tuning-up, incidentally, received rapturous applause.

The EP, featuring titles that said it all like "Blank Generation" and "You Gotta Lose", found Hell peddling fairly orthodox music-industry "nihilism" that, naturally, didn't prevent him from expounding his philosophy of the rejection of everything, everyone, everywhere into a long-playing record which, naturally, he felt sufficiently "nihilistic" about to promote on a European tour.

Actually, the most outrageously "nihilistic" occurrence of the marketing crusade was that potential punters took Hell at his "nihilistic" word and stayed home!

Though Hell was nearly famous for sporting a T-shirt bearing the courteous "nihilistic" legend "Please Kill Me", he whimpered for mercy when an obliging Newcastle punk aimed a firework at Hell's eyes.

Richard has since retreated from the taxing lifestyle of wandering "nihilistic" minstrel into the womb of New York socialising, spending his "nihilistic" days awaiting the arrival of a prestigious (and therefore obscure) European New Wave (no, honestly!) moviemaker.

Richard makes Gloria Swanson in *Sunset Boulevard* look like a Hot Property.

What's your film gonna be called, Richie?

Slowly, the starlet scratches his head. "I forgot to ask . . ."

How wonderfully "nihilistic", man.

Whereas Hell was attempting to perfect cynical inhumanity for the dubious benefit of artistic credibility, The Ramones were pushing the same product for motives of a purely financial kind.

The Ramones were formed in 1974 by four middle-class teenagers (in the mid-Sixties, that is) from the lush suburbia of New York's Forest Hills. Before changing their names, they had flicked their wrists in various chronic combos – no hope Heavy Metal hackbands and as such perfect apprenticeships for The Ramones own eventual perversion of "punk". The stage-brother's roll-call was spot-blitzed shaded short-ass Tommy "Pox Chops" Ramone on drums and Valderma; moon-featured round-shouldered Quasimodo-hunchbacked Johnny "Guitar" Ramone; one of Mother Nature's most tragic mistakes on vocals Joey "Who's A Pretty Boy Then?" Ramone, a decrepit inferno crippled with infirmities; and blank bassist Dee Dee "Stands For Deaf and Dumb" Ramone, pigeyed, pea-brained and fitting in perfectly with his brothers – and also Seymour Stein, head of Sire Records, the label which signed The Ramones just after Danny Fields became their manager at the end of 1975.

Dictionary definition of Sire: "father, forefather; male parent of beast, especially stallion; to beget, especially of stallions". Stein has also Sired saucy starlet Richard Hell and flouncing faggots The Dead Boys and, by a queer quirk of fate, the enigmatically estimable Talking Heads. These bands constituting around half of the New York punk elite, Seymour got more than he can use.

*Use* being the operative word in a city where the music industry has reached new heights of under-the-counter incest – the submission of journalism and snapshots for the artistes veto not an unusual occurrence, and banning from the prestigious CBGB portals on the whim of club owner Hilly Kristal a virtual censorship on access to an ostensibly live audience.

And even if a band make it onto the stage, they then have to survive the savage scrutiny of influential media magnates Richard Robinson (record producer/rock writer) and his sly spouse Lisa Robinson (syndicated scribe/socialite scene manipulator) – the only NYC hacks who call the tune when it comes to the submission of well-worn wares.

Seymour and his business (but not sleeping) partner-wife Linda control investment of capital, Richard and Lisa control media marketing, and the fun foursome share a collective court jester in senile whizz-kid Danny Fields, ex-hired hand of Lou Reed, The Stooges and The Doors – now handling the bewildered brothers.

Therefore it was hardly a heart-stopper to find a Sincere Message of Special Thanks to Seymour and Linda and Richard and Lisa on the back of The Ramones' first album, released in February 1976.

The music was sub-standard Heavy Metal fare cynically souped-up to a speedy buzz-saw drone that (predictably, as the band all wore leather jackets) passed for punk, while the literary content of the brothers Retard Rock showed a chronic arrestment of mentality suitable for four patriotic nephews of Uncle Sam who had wanted to go to Vietnam to "kill Chinks" but were unfortunately rejected for lacking the intellectual capacity America required of her My Lai war heroes.

Since Elvis first strolled into a studio to cut "How Great Thou Art" for his beloved Mom, pop-stars have pushed what are essentially stunted, soft-brained stances as pseudo-proof of their Eternal Youth. But The Ramones took the Peter "Pea Brain" Pan complex to unprecedented extremes with their war-comic Nazism, paeans to sick cinematic mass-murder gore, and feeble attempts to promote a youthful image with references to their dimmest memories of dating, dancing and pubescent drug abuse like glue-sniffing.

99 per cent of rock critics are from the same prune-featured generation as The Ramones, and only like bands which make them feel young again. So naturally the press went overboard and when The Ramones toured in the summer of '76, the Great British Punk Public were primed by the powers of auto-suggestion to lap up whatever the brothers deigned to spit at them.

In fact, the only saving grace of a Ramones gig was that if you popped out for a quick puke at the mezzanine celebration of a nation which invented the bomb to wipe out human life while leaving real estate intact, such was the austerity of the show that you stood a fair chance of missing it altogether! Though the mundane minimalism of The Ramones was lauded as the direct antithesis of all those so suddenly unfashionable Sixties Axe Heroes, the brothers were not revolutionary but reactionary.

Unlike the admittedly self-indulgent virtuosi with their thirty-minute guitar solos – who had at least genuinely cared about the music they were playing – the breakneck pace of The Ramones (33 songs during one hour in Seattle) was indicative of nothing more than their utmost contempt for their music, their audience and, justifiably, themselves.

The door-to-door salesman attitude, aiming to move as much merchandise with the smallest possible number of sales-drives, has permeated the rest of their career; British tours are never set up to give The Ramones a chance to play for their misguided fans, but to shift their latest product ... "Ramones Leave Home" released early 1977/tour spring '77/"Rocket To Russia" released late 1977/tour New Year '78.

But while The Ramones managed to cover their travelling expenses at the box-office, neither their three albums nor a string of persuasively picture-sleeved singles managed to make the slightest scratch on the charts either side of the Atlantic. Though the difference between middle-class, barbiturate-taking/dope-smoking, fatalistic American kids and working-class, drink-ing/speeding, bitter British kids is vast, they have something in common. They all want *bands that they can follow.*

In the UK, punks are prepared to pay out hard cash for expensive albums by bands who could just as easily have been standing behind them in an audience. Kids like themselves, the fact that they were musicians almost incidental, who maybe just a month ago had been standing next to them at the bar "down the Roxy". Kids who had followed these bands long before they had signed six-figure recording contracts (with companies that would have laughed at them had it not been for their hard-core, ready-made "market") not only felt like peers, but also like campaigners.

But American kids get everything on a plate, especially their recreation. After a decade of munching trash-food from foil plates while staring at their interminable Technicolor television brain-candy, pre-teen kids at Aerosmith, Kiss and Queen concerts are equipped for nothing more strenuous (especially after washing down the bare essentials of Quaalude-depressants with cheap wine) than being able to *focus on the stage.*

The gross majority of these audiences haul their asses off of a comfy air-conditioned couch and into a giant sports-stadium for the technoflash visual rather than the multi-decibel audio experience. They're not even studying the ant-size performers strutting a tiny stage half a mile away – they're there purely to be bludgeoned into the merciful cosmic oblivion of misplaced and mushy mysticism.

This stupid state of non-being is achieved by partaking of America's own inimitable cocktail of tranquillisers, the overwhelm-ing omnipotence of a Big Daddy (whether he be in the Whitehouse or on a stage) and, biggest and best of all, an awesome artificial Aurora Borealis electronically created by a blinding light-show of vivid laser-beams.

And even if these wondrous colours have been scientifically exposed as carriers of radio-activity, forcing a few states to introduce legislation restricting their wanton use, that's "the breaks, man", the chance a mere mortal takes when he gawps at his tin god. When the unlucky few realise that their complexion is suffering not from acne but from radiation, they probably wish they'd stayed at home sleeping with the TV on.

American rock and roll – very affluent, very crass, very much Television With Credibility.

But the kids just keep on buying the album of the light-show, because – goddamn – even if lasers and Quaaludes don't keep the doctor away, at least the way Aerosmith, Kiss and Queen constantly cross and re-cross America playing hundreds of gigs to millions of kids year after year – means they *care*!

The Ramones were Atlantic middle-men attempting to straddle two continents and consequently getting their balls broken by both sides. They had no eye-catching stage-shows, no tours unless there was a new product to push, no empathy with any community outside of New York City business circles.

The Ramones claim that the Thirties film *Freaks* by Todd Browning is their major influence. In fact, their attraction to the movie is probably far closer to identification than derivation.

Mink De Ville's attraction to the new wave is more monetary than hereditary, although their riffs are all borrowed from the cultures of America's disowned citizens – the blacks and Puerto Ricans. More than any other band-leader, Willy De Ville has slandered the journalists on whom he blames the phrase "Punk Rock", yet more than any other new USA combo, his band would never have made it beyond the S & M bars (as Billy De Sade And The Marquis) had it not been instantly-'76 hip to ape the wild and woolly antics of young dumb proles.

Mink De Ville were formed by the silly Willy of the same name in San Francisco 1972, though the first time anyone other than their Mamas paid any heed to them was when in 1976 they struck lucky and wheedled three track-marks out of that New York City turkey turning-point in "Punk", "Live At CBGB's", released on Atlantic.

Willy and his boys would have gone straight back to thrashing it out in the leather bars had not the biggest NYC New (and not quite so new) Wave names already been put on a reluctant retainer by other labels, leaving Capitol near-frantic as to where they would find their own token punks. Flicking through the "CBGB" sleeve (which served as a last-ditch roll-call of the bands which no one, not even Atlantic, would sign), a Capitol talent scout finally decided that, of all eight bands on the album, oldsters Tuff Darts looked and sounded the least hopeless.

However, in the flesh Tuff Darts proved too much of a musical anachronism to be considered for grooming with a view to stardom (even if they did wear short hair and skinny ties just like the Anglo punks) and the Capitol A & R man fell for the more malleable Mink De Ville on the rebound, signing them at the end of 1976.

The Rank Charm School never worked as many miracles on its gauche sow's-ears as Capitol did on theirs. With Mink De Ville playing Eliza Dolittle in the studio, Capitol went about the serious business of making an album; bringing in pianist Bobby Leonards, Phil Spector's saxophonist Steve Douglas, black trio of silk-suited soul-singers The Immortals and, somehow, persuading Jack Nitzsche to produce.

Forty-year-old Nitzsche had received his Diploma of Music nearly two decades ago before going to Hollywood to create Phil Spector's Wall Of Sound, writing, producing and arranging dozens of classic singles before turning his back on establishment rock and roll in 1972 to concentrate on film soundtracks. His work on the Mink De Ville album was not an apology to Youth Culture for rejecting its chosen messenger, rather it was an affirmation of his total contempt for rock and roll.

Willy De Ville: "Jack saw the whole thing as a movie, man."

Nitzsche saw his masterpiece as the backdrop to the greatest story never told; De Ville saw the whole thing as B-feature beach-party remake of *West Side Story*, where human beings with warts and emotions were reduced to the level of cardboard cutouts with switchblades and halos – surrogate Fonzies in the mould of bad-ass Bruce Springsteen (who had himself stolen it from Tim Buckley) street-romanticism.

Nitzsche knew too much not to put a merciful end to the self-important guitar-screech and drum-drone of orthodox Rock, mixing them into a tasteful oblivion. Instead, he showcased the delicacy of Douglas' saxophone, Leonards' piano and a xylophone which De Ville considered too fey to list on the album credits – a musical landscape ordained not for Willy's warbling *ordinaire* but for the soft-focus harmonies of The Immortals, with their angelic echoes of Smokey's Miracles, which earned them their very own Capitol recording contract.

Predictably, when the album "Mink De Ville" (which De Ville, predictably, wished to call "Cabretta" – meaning 'tough but tender leather'!) was released in the spring of 1977, overawed critics couldn't tell their Jack from their Willy. And inevitably, their ecstatic ejaculation proved to be premature when the band toured the UK in autumn – supporting pub-rock warhorses Dr Feelgood.

The audience went along to see the stage show of the movie – sorry, *album* – but what they got was only rock'n'roll, and they didn't like it, like it, no they didn't. Jack Nitzsche couldn't make it tonight, gang, but he sent his session-men instead!

Disregarding Willy De Ville's extravagant slicked-backed pompadour coiffure and his "fruity" (his word) purple platform boots, the water-tight proof of the singer's Potsie-type *Happy Days* credibility was when he responded to your humble authors' wizard jape of threatening to end Mink De Ville's career if we didn't get a free copy of the album – by flying two Lower East Side hit-men over to London!

They sought us here, they sought us there, because we're pretty irreverent and we don't care!

Remember, Willy, what your hero Stephen Sondheim almost said?

"When you're a Wet you're a Wet all the way/From your first cigarette till your last dying day!"

While every other pretender to CBGB barspace had needed to shake off their hometowns before changing their surnames and muttering about "getting a band together", Talking Heads were already a whole when they arrived in NYC in the autumn of 1974. They played their first gig the following summer as the only unit whose musicians had not suffered differences of artistic opinion while working in other bands currently making the rounds.

Tina Weymouth, Chris Frantz and David Byrne first became a co-operative in 1973 at the Rhode Island School of Design in the town of Providence, when bored and rich, Frantz (drums) and Byrne (guitar/vocals) formed a band called The Artistics, aided by cheer-leading admiral's daughter Tina. At this point their music was more cold-hearted collegiate nihilism in the mouldy mould of Verlaine and Hell, The Artistics and Tina working on songs like "Psycho Killer (*Qu'est ce-que c'est?*)" and "Sick Boy" until Byrne dropped out of college a year later to work in an art gallery while the other two stayed on to get their degrees.

Thus equipped, they packed their guitars and diplomas in an old kitbag and set out to see if the streets of New York City really were paved with poets. Working on their day-jobs, the two Artistics brought Tina in on bass and Talking Heads played their first gig in the summer of 1975, supporting The Ramones at CBGB's.

They played regularly at CBGB's and would probably still be strutting their stuff in front of tablefuls of cool customers (covertly clock-watching for the moment when the club's ushers would shoo them out to make way for a new batch) had it not been for the Anglo-inspired punk-rush of late 1976, when Talking Heads were signed to Sire.

It said something for Talking Heads' sound New England background that they're the only hallowed American '70s band never to have sacked anyone. Jerry Harrison had left another New England band, Jonathan Richman's Modern Lovers, totally disillusioned with the music business, to work as a teacher but felt sufficient empathy to Talking Heads to sit in (on guitar, keyboards and second vocals) on several of their gigs. After the band secured a contract, he was persuaded to throw in his full-time lot with Talking Heads, just in time for their spring tour of the UK, supporting (again) Sire-stable-mates The Ramones.

Critical response to Talking Heads was favourable, though never approaching the religious ecstasy with which the wrinkled hacks greeted the wretched Ramones. Untouched by public approval, Talking Heads just got on with what they wanted to do – recording their debut album and leaving it in the can while Tina Weymouth and Chris Frantz got married in his hometown of Maysville, Kentucky (population 500) in July 1977. The bride wore white, the music was stereophonic and Chris Frantz said: "We've been living together for three years, and we thought 'Let's show that we're serious'."

The album "Talking Heads '77" was released in autumn, and although musically the band were the most refreshing of all the American acts, with a clean, subtle and infectious sound reminiscent of vintage Stax Veda Brown's "Shortstoppin'", shrill, whining Byrne is too much a song-writer who feels he has to sing his baby safely through the album.

The only thing that made Byrne any different from every other singer-songwriter who had taken so much weight on his shoulders that his legs were buckling was the frame of reference he used. Whereas every other band's lyrics promoted the image of a non-existent sub-stratum of society (The Heartbreakers' glamorous junkies; The Ramones' lovable pinheads; Television's profound visionaries; Mink De Ville's sensitive hoodlums and Richard Hell's martyred nihilists), Byrne's lyrics dealt with nothing but the day-to-day confluence of life revolving around everyman's preoccupations of home, job, family, friends, loved ones and civil servants.

Their inscrutable isolation may have entranced the critics, but it was hardly the stuff from which either punk esoteria or platinum albums are made, and "Talking Heads '77" plus a succession of singles all failed to figure in the charts. Undeterred, the band played 20 headlining English dates at the start of 1978.

The futility of their labour became apparent when Talking Heads revealed the identity of their next producer, a decision indicating that they are destined to become nothing more than the latest lame-dog (after Ultravox and *Jubilee*) of ex-Bryan Ferry Band-man Baldwin Eno.

It took New York City to rot the brain behind Talking Heads; it took California, that other hub of the music industry/twin armpit of the USA, to incapacitate their fellow New Englander, Jonathan Richman.

Richman was born in Boston and formed his band The Modern Lovers in 1970 at the age of nineteen "because I was lonely". Musically, the band improved on the bludgeoning riff repetition of Richman's beloved fave raves, The Velvet Underground and The Stooges, while his lyrics reflected a healthy contempt for Lou and Iggy's whining and wallowing in self-hating squalor. Instead, he sang about the fact that inhumanity can *never* be blamed on environment ("Roadrunner" and "Modern World"), easy respect for parents and the past, making a mockery of the Generation Gap ("Old World") and a monogamous chivalry which showed all those 50s/60s/70s "Two Girls For Every Boy" macho closet-cases up for what they were/are/will be ("Hospital", "Someone I Care About", "Astral Plane" and "Girlfriend").

When The Modern Lovers delivered their anti-depressant song "I'm Straight" to zomboid audiences who habitually swallowed Quaaludes like they were Smarties, the band were showered with bottles and rotten fruit by soft-brained campussers irritated by the fact that Richman's was a selective and informed censorship – of promiscuity but not of sex, of dehumanising drugs but not of illegal though harmless stimulants; the only moral morality there is.

Such a bright young band, doomed for neither the oblivion of office-jobs nor the complacency of success, proved too much for John Cale (founder of The Velvet Underground and now corporation talent-scout), who signed them to Warner Brothers for $100,000 in 1973. He gloated over his conquest by taking them to record in California.

The Modern Lovers could not have met a crueller fate even if John Cale had choreographed it, when by the end of the year the extortionate oil prices of greedy Arabs agitated such a chronic vinyl shortage that every record company was forced to keep new product to an absolute minimum. Many talented unknowns were unceremoniously sacked by budgeting labels, including The Modern Lovers from Warner Brothers.

Cut off in their prime 3,000 miles from home with no label and, more important, no claim to the tentative debut album tapes (unarguably the apex of Lou Reed, Iggy Pop and Jonathan Richman's careers), The Modern Lovers scattered. Richman returned to Boston at the start of 1974, too bitter to become anything but a bad businessman. He sniffed half-heartedly after another recording contract and occasionally ventured onstage backed only by a bunch of kids beating rolled-up newspapers, before disappearing for long spells locked in his bedroom.

In 1975 a new West Coast label called Beserkley took pity on him, and signed him as their all-purpose patron fruitcake. Jonathan cobbled together The Modern Lovers Mark two, who did what was required of them for the spring 1976 album "Jonathan Richman And The Modern Lovers", an acoustic betrayal of all that Richman had held dear. The new Jon-Jon raised its gurgling head for the first time, revealing that the erstwhile Modern Lover had retained his ideal of moral purity (*après le* rude awakening) only by retreating into the cosy womb of songs like "Abominable Snowman In The Supermarket", "Here Come The Martian Martians" and (who's a cheeky boy, then?) "Hey There Little Insect".

This excuse for a $33\frac{1}{3}$ r.p.m. product, depicting Jonathan chuckling merrily away in his shiny new padded cell, might have slipped by unnoticed had not Beserkley persuaded Warner Brothers to part with their *original* Modern Lovers tapes. In a piece of monumental mismanagement, Beserkley released these tapes as an album entitled "The Modern Lovers" a few weeks before the marketing of their home-grown item.

"The Modern Lovers" seemed like the first record on which the menacingly glamorous side of rock had been integrated into lyrics asserting a healthy outlook on life. His brain rotting steadily away, Richman has spent his subsequent career trying to live down toppling the established bourgeois immorality of "rock'n'roll" ("I don't want some cocaine-sniffing triumph in a bar/I don't want a triumph in a car/I don't want to make a rich girl crawl/All I want is a girl that I care about/Or I want no one at all/Alright, listen to this now!") to replace it with something immeasurably better.

From his Beserkley betrothal to this day (refusing as he does to discuss the potentially frightening subject of what happened to the boy who cut the most innovatory record in the history of rock), Richman's sole message has been: "WHO'S THE BIGGEST SUCKER – YOU OR ME?"

"Rock'n'Roll With The Modern Lovers", released in the autumn of 1976, found Jonathan experimenting with a drummer beating on a hub-cap in a ladies toilet, while on his first UK tour (recorded for a live album released at the end of the year) Richman delighted the multitudes by opening his set with five consecutive renditions of "Ice Cream Man", imitating an aeroplane on "I'm A Little Aeroplane" and getting down on all fours for a song called "Little Dinosaur".

Whatever his morbid motives, the general public were sold, sending his three singles "Roadrunner", "Egyptian Reggae" and "Morning Of Our Lives" into the Top Twenty, and commercial success served as the final shove down into the 5-star asylum of opulent safe idiocy.

American bands are old and cold and still coming to terms with the fact that the Sixties ran out on them. Their acid-tinted cosmic romanticism stomped into the ploughed-up festival-site mud at the turn of the decade, they seem determined not to get fooled again, determined never to put anyone or anything before their bank-account.

Or as one old hippie (now leader of a successful USA Heavy Metal glitter band) sums it up: "I'LL DO ANYTHING FOR OUR AUDI-ENCE. I'LL KISS THEIR ASS IF ONLY THEY'LL BUY OUR ALBUMS. THEN, WHEN WE'VE SOLD A MILLION, I'LL SHIT OVER EVERY-ONE!!!"

But the more *dedicated* American *punk* bands attribute their indifference to everything but their own whimsical wanks not to fiscal ambition, but to their membership of what they like to call "The Blank Generation". Tom Verlaine's poems may have given Richard Hell a thrill, but they didn't pay his bills – so Richie went back to college to grab a diploma in despondency and composed the anthem of the out-of-sync home-movie which all new Ameri-can bands took to their blank hearts: "I belong to the Blank Genera-tion and I can take it or leave it each time – take it!"

"Ah, America", sighs Gore Vidal. "Love it or leave it. . . ."

Gore has lived in Italy for sixteen years.

# DRUGS

Time was when a minstrel's main motivations towards the trappings of success were hunger pains for unlimited supplies of fame, finance and flesh-pots. As early as 1955, an unknown 20-year-old called Elvis Aaron Presley out of Tupelo, Mississippi, was honouring the tradition of his hard-slogging Country and Western neighbours by using large quantities of amphetamine pills as an extension of the bare essentials of food and sleep – to provide the stamina necessary to survive the gruelling rigours of interminable one-nighter tours of the Southlands.

A God-fearing, red-blooded boy who loved his mother, Elvis used amphetamines (a pharmaceutical which by stimulating the central nervous system produces euphoria, self-confidence, energy, alertness and endurance) in a functional, sensible, righteous manner. But by the time he was a legendary, still-warm corpse over two decades later, those who would be kings were not taking drugs so they could work. They were working so that they could take drugs.

The two costly chemicals that bands (Americans, with the exception of two or three irretrievably Stateside English smack-exiles) are Working Their Way Through Rock for are heroin and cocaine.

At £70 a gram, heroin is the drug which costs you the most and gives you the least. On a capable, rebellious individual, heroin has the dulling effect of a second-rate sleeping-pill. To a sadly-lacking sub-Superman type, heroin seems to be the safely sexless "kick"; not the narcotic itself – impoverished junkies often inject mere water into their veins – but the feel of *that needle going in!*

It takes a conscious, continuous decision to become a junkie – addiction to heroin requires a hardened addict's bare essential of half a grain every day for a fortnight – and, therefore, those who choose this route cannot be pitied or excused. The junkie is driven down by wanting to be someone "special" a.k.a. shot-through with self-hatred, puritanism and a failing to come to terms with the fact that he is a human animal.

Besides being the only 24-hour shift which soaks up every penny you have (in England, only aristocrats and Arabs are rich/stupid enough to fall for it), heroin addiction brings one bonuses such as constant drowsiness, impotence, constipation and the slow but sure need for a steadily mounting dose.

The only rock stars who openly admit to taking heroin nowadays (Iggy and Lou, who built their careers around the white crystals, having since "cleaned up" for a public consumption which never happened) are fresh-faced Rolling Stone Keef "Is Guilty" Richard – who discovered that the Mounties always wait for their man when they busted him for trafficking heroin! – and petite Power-Pop chanteuse Debbie Blondie, the solitary heroin PR of new wave showbiz.

"I hated touring in Australia, although 'In The Flesh' was number one for two weeks there. The best thing about the place was the smack."

The heroin bands are based on the East Coast of America, producing raw, abrasive noise before opting for cute, commercial compromise. The mistake the record-buying public make, while nodding off to the silky, bland, blonde sound churned out by their unimpeachable West Coast favourites, is assuming that this muzak-with-credibility is inspired by sun and surf, and not cocaine.

Cocaine is the oldest anaesthetic known to man – first given by the Incas to sacrificial victims about to have their hearts cut out – now much favoured by ex-hippies who have suddenly decided that they'd better get Seventies if they want to get rich. As it has never been fashionable since the Roaring Twenties, cocaine is a hip-wimp drug, and people like Linda Ronstadt, Fleetwood Mac and The Eagles indulge in it with a clear, melodic conscience.

The anaesthetising properties of cocaine have been peddled by the powers of auto-suggestion as being an aphrodisiac and a stimulant of creative faculties – the two attributes calculated to make impotent, uninspired musicians (and others) reach feverishly for their American Express cards.

Another attraction cocaine has to the West Coast Mrs Millses for teenagers in their mid-twenties is that, unlike heroin, it is not addictive. Or as one Los Angeles pop star puts it: "You just can't get hooked on coke, man. Really. I've been using it for nearly twelve years and I'm *still* not addicted." Cocaine is usually cut up into thin white lines and sniffed up through a small tube. Habitual use eats away the bone partition between the nostrils, which must be surgically replaced with a non-corrosive metal. Linda Ronstadt is just one Californian nightingale with a golden voice and a silver nose.

But although expensive surgery can go some way to saving the snout of a long-term coke freak, no amount of royalty cheques can spare users the various other side-effects like gruesome hallucinations, paranoid delusions, breathing failure and brain paralysis.

Cocaine is not a narcotic like alcohol, and not physically addictive like heroin, as dependence on coke lies in the mind and not the body. Jerry Brown, Governor of California, staunch Roman Catholic, and steady date of Linda Ronstadt, has taken the initial steps towards decriminalising cocaine in the same way that marijuana possession has been made as inconsequential as a parking-ticket. These days, the California judicial system only threatens to come down hard on coke criminals who have information they want – as in the case of Anjelica Huston, an actress who testified that her close friend film director Roman Polanski had taken a 13-year-old girl into a bedroom. Her revelation caused her possession of cocaine charge to be dropped, and forced Polanski to plead guilty. See how he runs ... when the Feds catch up with you, Roman, we hope they cut off your tail with a carving knife.

As downhome farmer Carter drawls that marijuana should be decriminalised nationwide, the smart set have decided that dope is peanuts, moving onto cocaine at approximately £1,100 an ounce. Their whims are catered to by the poverty-ridden peasants of South America – it's Colombia's biggest export, butting a fellow caffeine-derivative, coffee, into second place. Americans spend £2,000 million annually on cocaine.

One British rock star who defected to California keeps a goldfish bowlful of cocaine – worth about £200,000 – in his gold-plated bathroom. His choice of container displays a remarkable humility when compared to the profusion of lavish paraphernalia produced to give the use of cocaine an atmospheric ambience akin to a Japanese hari-kari ritual – the original method of sniffing the drug off a mirror with a rolled up bank-note being far too accessible for the coke snobs.

*Tiffany's* sell silver cocaine-sniffing straws at nine dollars each; *Maxferd's*, a San Francisco jeweller's, stock cocaine spoons made of precious metals and encrusted with gems; the Hollywood shop *Propinquity* offers solid gold cocaine kits from $4,500.

These arrogant accessories are bought by West Coast musicians with cocaine running around their rotted brains, as they go about their business of being mid-thirties Middle Of The Road hepcats. Almost without exception, these cracked actors spent the Sixties preaching revolution via d-Lysergic Acid Diethylamide, and that third-rate tranquilliser cannabis.

Acid (as it came to be known, man) was an inward-bound experience for cosmic cretins born too early to queue up for *Star Wars*. But once light shows, Yankee comics, *Star Trek* and Day-Glo denim became public property, dropping acid was on a social etiquette par with wetting the bed.

Smoking dope causes dulling of attention, sluggishness, silliness, a mouth that tastes like a Turk's turd, and increases the appetite to such proportions that prolonged smoking results in gross obesity.

Marijuana would never have become as inevitable as stereophonic sound to rock music, had it not helped to perpetuate the mood of affluent complacence prevalent in the Sixties (whose culture has since clung like a monkey on the shoulder) and been nurtured in the Seventies by a cult of Jamaican religious fanatics, the Rastafarians, whose stoned sexist/racist/mystic gospel has been welcomed with open wallets by the white ex-hippie entrepreneurs who, before they converted to the capitalist faith, believed in very much the same doctrine as the Rastas.

The bastion of all that is philistine about rock and roll is the American glossy *Rolling Stone.* This dope-smoker's *Reader's Digest* was started in 1967 by three old men to document hippie ideology and, true to form, in the Seventies, has served the function of acting as a limp PR organ for the entire contingent of West Coast coke scum.

In 1977 *Rolling Stone* celebrated its tenth anniversary with a TV special in which Las Vegas go-go dancers gyrated to an orchestrated Beatles medley. Back in the days when the magazine was cryptically extolling the virtues of dope and acid, it printed instructions on how to make Molotov cocktails – for the sole purpose of throwing them at dealers of amphetamines.

Understandable, because amphetamine – the only drug that makes you sit up and ask questions rather than lie down and lap up answers – is the only drug not to act as an all-American palliative. Dope, downers, LSD, cocaine and heroin – they all demand "Thou shalt have no other God before me", whereas speed does nothing more than act as a hyper-active vitamin pill.

While rock and roll beats its chest about fathering the Dope Culture and the Acid Culture, turns a blind eye to downers, and winks knowingly at cocaine whilst acknowledging that "Heroin" (even if junkies, poor fools, are to be pitied) is one of the greatest counter-culture songs ever written, it steers superstitiously clear of the dread speed.

Because it is a *useful* drug; 72 million tablets taken by British troops in the second world war, and used by doctors since 1932 to treat epilepsy, alcoholism, schizophrenia, problem children, neurotic housewives, over-worked men, heart block, migraine, head injuries, nearly every form of drug addiction and much, much more including nettle-rash.

Because it is a *threatening* drug; it increases the IQ by an average of eight points and (if snorted and not injected) is not addictive, except in persons desperate for something to blame their deficiencies on – the speed user either finds a sensible dose or cracks up.

And because, unlike dope and acid which were never anything more than *youth* (so long as the youth had been to college, that is) drugs, speed has always been an essentially *proletarian* drug. When the Mods discovered that amphetamines totally complemented their lifestyle in the early 1960s, it was because they were working-class and in need of a stimulant which would not stop them from earning a living – that they were young was a convenient incidental.

The Mods set their own standards, and used their drugs instead of letting their drugs use them. Amphetamines aided and abetted them in dancing, dressing and speeding – stimulated not intoxicated, aware not doped/drunk/defeated – through the 60 hours of a Mod weekend.

Of the Mod bands, the manufactured Who sang their melodramatic fantasies of what they imagined the amphetamine lifestyle to be and reached a credulous mass audience, while the Small Faces were the archetype who had lived the life before they were ever in a band. In "Here Comes The Nice" they said more in three minutes about Mod than Pete Townshend said in thirty years.

"Here comes the nice/Looking so good/Make me feel like no one else could/Knows what I want/Got what I need/Always there when I need some speed."

Like Mod, the life-blood of punk was finally contaminated into an industry by slumming, exploiting middle-class leeches. And their shared patron drug, so potentially subversive, became nothing more than the apt attitude to adopt.

From the demi-gods to the dregs, anyone not in the Ex Pistols has embraced the persona of a "speed freak" in much the same way as they would have thrown themselves into the part of laid-back "flower child" (pretending to be stoned) had their bands been begat ten years earlier.

Significantly, the only punk face to be busted for speed was the one who single-handedly instigated the movement: Johnny Rotten. Appropriately, speed is the only drug which acts as a spur; the only social mobility drug. It is the only drug that can make a prole realise that to *make it* you don't need more intelligence, just the confidence to flaunt that sharpness in the faces of those who would have dismissed you because of your background, the confidence to look down on *them.* Speed is the only thing that can take the place of elocuation lessons.

And, as Johnny's mum put it when interviewed about the apple of her eye getting caught: "It was only speed – it wasn't a *hard* drug!"

Mother knows best.

# GIRLS

The role of women in rock and roll is best summed up by that female impersonator supreme, Iggy Pop –

"I've been dirt – and I don't care."

Party line of the late Sixties ("Revolution for everyone who's not a woman, man") women who played the role of victim-in-long-skirt sitting on a kitchen stool crying onto a strictly non-electric guitar. And, awesome as they were, those early Sixties soul-girls were nothing more than moron-mouthpieces for ugly men with no voice.

It took the sound sense of the Seventies to nurture the few rock and roll women worthy of the gender – Nico, Fanny, Labelle and the magnificent Suzi Quatro. The Mega-Stars of glitter-glam may have been outrageously outspoken about their sexual preferences within the safe sanctuary of interviews, but when it came to marketable product they played it anything but piebald. They compensated, as male rock stars had always done, with songs aimed to kill at girls.

Punk rock in 1976 was the first rock and roll phase *ever* not to insist that women should be picturesque topics and targets of songs; punks were too hung up on tower-blocks to be power-driven cock-of-the-walk. Never before has there been less lee-way for women who persist in kow-towing to *men*. Nevertheless, the only women who have not gone under are Joan Jett, Tina Weymouth, Pauline Noname and Poly Styrene.

Blessed with the finest imagination of her generation, Poly Styrene (born Marion Elliot) has disregarded social handicaps (race, sex and class) which anyone else would have built a career around (Rastafarians, Runaways and Resentful Rebels).

"You are just a concept/You are just a dream/You're just a reflection of the new regime/You are just a symbol/You are just a theme/You're just another figure for the sales machine/You are just a victim/You are just a find/Soon to be a casualty/A casualty of time/OOOH-OOOH!/OBSESSED WITH YEW-OOOH!"

Born of a white mother and a black father into the unbearable hostility of Brixton, Poly Styrene tried to live alternately as a black and a white for fifteen years before being forced by racial cross-fire to run away from London and hitch around the country, alone.

"Identity is the crisis, cantcha see?/When you look in the mirror do you see yourself?/Do you see yourself on a TV screen?/Do you see yourself in a magazine?/When you see yourself does it make you scream?/When you look in the mirror do you smash it quick?/Do you take the glass and slash your wrists?/Did you do it for fame?/Did you do it in a fit?/Did you do it before you read about it?/Identity is the crisis, cantcha see?"

Upon returning to London, Poly earned a living from running her own stall (called *X-Ray Spex*) in King's Road's Beaufort Market, making and selling her own clothes designs "to art students". In January 1977 she stopped treading water and formed a band called X-Ray Spex: "I don't know how – I just did! It was just that time when anybody could form a band." And fortunately for Poly and her backing band, it was just that time when anyone could be recorded for the Roxy album – in this instance, X-Ray Spex prime cut "Oh Bondage! Up Yours!" being pinned down for posterity on their second ever gig.

As EMI had used its Roxy bands as a one-off hit or tax-loss, so the Virgin label – ever slow to second a trend – took on X-Ray Spex for a single's-worth of a groomed studio version of the album track. "Oh Bondage! Up Yours!" was banned by the BBC and salivated over by the national and counter-culture press as "a song about bondage". Released in the autumn of 1977, it was a song about pride.

"Bind me tie me chain me to the wall/I wanna be a slave to you all/Oh Bondage! Up Yours!/Oh Bondage! No More!/Oh Bondage! Up Yours!/Oh Bondage! No More!/Chain store chain smoke I consume you all/Chain gang chain mail I don't think at all/Trash me crash me beat me till I fall/I wanna be a victim for you all/Oh Bondage! Up Yours!/Oh Bondage! No More!/Oh Bondage! Up Yours!/Oh Bondage! NO MORE!"

The way the frightened press deliberately misconstrued the anti-oppression song into a pro-repression message was reflected in their attitude to Poly herself. Pretty, personable but determinedly asexual onstage, Poly was attacked by threatened male critics for having a brace, a brain and no visible boyfriend.

"I know I'm artificial/But don't put the blame on me/I was reared with appliances in a consumer society/In a consumer society/When I put on my make-up/My pretty little mask is not me/It's just the way a girl should be in a consumer society/In a consumer society/Wanna be Instamatic/Wanna be a frozen pea/Wanna be de-hydrated/In a consumer society."

Out of Virgin hands after Poly refused to play ball with the company and record cute lickle girl ads for the single, X-Ray Spex became the first punk band to show the Yankees who won the war when they were flown over to play six sell-out dates at that prestigious shrine CBGB's by the club's owner, Hilly Kristal.

As every punk band bolstered by record company money, outrageous reputations and chart albums had gone down Stateside like a lead lemming, pretty Poly and her boys came marching home to a heroes welcome, signing a recording contract with EMI in the spring of 1978 and becoming the first punk band to be given their own label.

All those pampered middle-class Americans who call themselves poets are not fit to lick the dreadlocks of the only singer whose lyrics can stand the test of transference onto cold, hard paper – Poly Styrene.

"I clambered up the miles and miles of Polystyrene foam/Then fell into a swimming pool filled with Fairy Snow/I wrenched the nylon curtains back as far as they would go/Then peered through perspex windows at the acrid orange glow/I drove my Poly-property car so far on wheels of rubber sponge/Then pulled into a Wimpy bar to have a rubber bun/The Day The World Turned Day-Glo/The Day The World Turned Day-Glo/The Day The World Turned Day-Glo/Oh-oh!"

Poly's vivid word-portraits of consumer fantasy gone mad justified their existence when X-Ray Spex decided which side they were on and joined the breeding-like-rabbits ranks of musicians who realise that politics are inseparable from life. At the start of the year, X-Ray Spex played the Roundhouse benefit for the National Abortion Campaign, crowning their commitment with the Trafalgar Square Anti-Nazi Rally followed by a show-of-strength march to Victoria Park, East London, for a carnival which included live music provided by The Tom Robinson Band, Steel Pulse and X-Ray Spex.

"Dark and eerie and it's really late/Come on, kid, don't hesitate/We're going down to the underground/The hate is lethal and dressed to kill/Tension heightening, hear it frightening/If you got the urge/Come on, let's submerge/Modern Order suffocate us/Smoulder on to obliterate us/If you got the urge/Come on, let's submerge."

You don't have to be black or a girl to hate fascism ... but it helps.

Unlike that white girl high on fascist-flirtation Siouxsie Sioux, who achieved transient fame as the *Sun* centre-spread pin-up punkette, though the apex of her rags-to-rags story happened when she played verbal footsie with Bill Grundy for a few seconds during the infamous Sex Pistols *Today* show. After that, it was down-hill all the way and Siouxsie was a never-was at 21.

Back in the good old days when she was a go-go dancer for The Pistols, Siouxsie twisted by the side of the stage decked out in her black leather peek-a-boo brassiere, swastika arm-band and fishnet pantaloons, until Malcolm decided to drop the Pan's Pistols schtick and poor S.S. – no chicken herself – was rendered redundant.

The S.S. girl found herself in the S.S. (Social Security) queue alongside another Rotten reject Sid Vicious (unemployed drummer), and on the re-bound they formed a combo called Siouxsie And The Banshees with the help of two guitar-picking cronies.

Sid soon left to be replaced by another loser, but Siouxsie's songs – "Metal", "Suburban Relapse", "Helter Skelter" (rumour has it that Siouxsie Is A Rutle Rocker), "Carcass" and "Love In A Void" (which contains the typical line "Too many Jews for my liking") – are still inspired by horror films, Charles Manson and nastiness in general to a back-drop of chain-store beer-keller muzak.

Despite being a suburban mother-lover who still rooms with her silver-haired mater, Siouxsie does not let her love of family life interfere with the serious task of bread-winning, and The Banshees toured constantly for two years *après* punk, until Polydor took pity on them in the summer of 1978.

Everything The Slits do, they do it about a month after Siouxsie does it (with the notable exception of securing a recording contract). They even carry not one, but two locks of Ex Pistols' hair around in their *Sex* handbags!

Ariana (public school, lead vocals, tantrums and John Rotten), Vivien (art school, lead guitar, Sidney Vicious and Mick Jones a.k.a. meal-ticket to support on Clash tour), Palmolive (drummer and Strummer) and Tessa (bass) perform not so much music as aural posturing designed to elevate them above the posing punkette *ordinaire.*

Any other band who couldn't carry a tune and couldn't get a recording contract would be tossing and turning all night, but The Slits sleep as snug as smug bugs in a rug. Because, coincidentally, their whole dalliance with show-business has been courtesy of Ariana's mother – a German newspaper heiress who looks like Ariana's own offspring!

The Great British Punk Sex Symbol (sing if you're glad to be it, Gaye) aside, the only UK girls left are The Rezillos' Fay Fife and Penetration's Pauline Noname – who are both so well integrated into their respective bands that their sex seems superfluous.

Fay is the PVC-polka-dotted-mini-skirted girl whose gender so offended Debbie "Dumb" Blondie that Deb vetoed The Rezillos as her support act on Blondie's first head-lining British gigs – though wethinks, perchance, t'was the tender years of this Fay wench that did weigh most heavily on the wrinkled shoulders of yon Harry. . . .

Parenthetically, another bunch of damn Yankees – The Ramones – were shaken in their smelly sneakers after being consistently blown offstage by the magic charm of Fay's cutting clowns when they supported De Blockhead Bruvvers on their New Year 1978 tour of these isles. The Ramones were so patently aware of The Rezillos superiority that for their important London gigs, the sublime Scots were relegated to the bottom of the three-band bill.

Penetration are a respected old-wave punk band, and this is due entirely to the distinctive, smooth, soulful, slick English voice of Pauline Noname – who unfortunately is oft reduced to screeching like a frenzied fishwife by the fairly orthodox repetitive bitching of Penetration.

Pauline's best bet would be to take her musicians out of circulation for a year or two until punk is nothing more than nostalgia-music, and then display that extraordinary soaring, searing voice to the public afresh.

Gaye Advert's backroom-boys, however, could never benefit from anything as mild as a couple of years in the cooler. Ever since her band began warming up the audience for various Roxy regulars at the start of 1977, poor Gaye Atlas has single-handedly served as the British new wave sex symbol as well as shouldering the ever-sagging career of those bandwagon blimps, Gaye's Adverts.

Then a beautiful brunette, Gaye was the one wheel which kept her Adverts trundling through their initial recording (a Stiff single, the promotion of which consisted of Gaye being "raffled" by limp-top-fat-cat Andrew Jakeman-Riviera) in the spring of 1977, which won them their Anchor recording contract soon after, whose appearance on *Top Of The Pops* rocketed Gaye's Adverts single "Gary Gilmore's Eyes" into the Top Twenty that summer (to be followed, as Gaye's looks were ravaged by drugs, by a string of 45 flops), and which finally drove Anchor to release Gaye's Adverts artistic masterpiece of an album "Crossing The Red Sea With Gaye's Adverts" (which, incredibly, was ignored) in early 1978.

Throughout her musical career, Gaye's way with a bass has been bypassed (by all papers with the exception of the *New Musical Express*) in favour of her filler-value as a standing joke whenever any gap appeared in a gossip column. Therefore, ex-music paper *Sounds* pounced like a vulture on a corpse when Eric Fuller, misogynist staff member of *Fiesta* pornographic magazine, dug up old pictures of Gaye posing as an 18-year-old called "Mella".

True to form, *Sounds* invented a reader's letter as an excuse to make Gaye's previous career known to the record-buying public – rewarding Fuller with a staff do.

In the spring of 1978, Gaye's Adverts replaced their original drummer. Also in the spring of 1978, Gaye's Adverts replaced their replacement.

They are not a happy band, and a split seems imminent; Gaye and her Advert's vocalist fight constantly and her guitarist is an aged gentleman almost ready to be pensioned off.

Gaye's American counterpart/ancestor is Debbie Blondie, with whom she has in common a band who sell themselves solely on her photogenic false-value, an affluent background from which she has made a deliberate and masochistic dive to the depths of "glamour modelling" and intravenous drug-taking and – most significantly – a boyfriend who has cadged a ride in on her personal popularity.

Gaye's beau (Gaye's Adverts vocalist and songwriter) sees himself as a sensitive seer, the veritable Poet Laureate of the new wave, allowing his steady-artist's mistress to be photographed cuddling up to small-time musicians as gossip-column quips, as a suitable way of getting his visionary poesy over to an audience who only look at the pictures. Debbie's old man (Blondie's guitarist) fancies himself – although nobody else does – as an international photographer of Scavullo proportions, and regards his growing portfolio of Deb pictured with the superstars as his ticket to the top. The glossy, professional way in which *this* boy hires out his girl-friend bids much brighter bread-winning prospects than Mr Adverts' tactics.

Mr Blondie describes the selling of Debbie thus as he offers up the famed leopard-skin leotard shots: "We had a really good run on this one. . . ."

With protectors like these, who needs critics?

After Debbie (then a short brunette) had stayed on at private school for as long as she could, she left New Jersey for the bright lights of New York City in the mid Sixties, and joined a band of rancid hippies called The Wind In My Willows. It was a bummer when the band split up, and Debbie divided her time for four years between being a junkie, a hostess and a hooker until, in the early Seventies, she graduated to Max's Kansas City as a groupie.

In 1971, Debbie (by now a shorter blonde) and a couple of other musicians' playthings formed garbage band The Stilettoes, which by 1973 had mutated into an infant Blondie – of which Debbie was the focal point, having thrown the other two female Stilettoes out of the band and changed the name. After numerous personnel and persona changes, Blondie had evolved a sufficiently "streets" sound by the end of 1976 to be signed by the shoestring-budget record label Private Stock. Their first album "Blondie" was released at the start of 1977 to an ignorant public who felt nothing at all.

It was the only album ever released on which every song could/should have been a hit single. Every last track was a pop classic, soft-focus cameo clarity skimming the waterfront of a blonde's lifestyle – surfing, vice raps, gang warfare, Chinese girls, giant ants and cat-fights. They could all survive on the juke-box jungle (what higher praise?), but they fell on deaf ears and lobo-tomised brains when Blondie supported the pathetic Television in the spring of 1977 and when a string of singles were released from the album.

But Blondie were the only band worth the entry fee even if you made your excuses and left before the main act slunk onstage to thunderous applause. They were the only American band yet who came here to *entertain* people rather than to carve that all-important *English* notch on their guitars (American artists being as angry as they are of being banana republic novices when it comes to rock and roll), but more important, Debbie was coolly contemptuous of the vociferous hecklers cat-calling because she was proud and feisty, as she rejected the servile role her gender are condemned to – especially in rock.

The first sign that Debbie had pawned pride for pounds and pence came in the autumn of 1977 when Chrysalis ("They are concerned for our future") bought Blondie from Private Stock ("They didn't take us seriously") for half a million dollars.

Just before Blondie headlined their first British tour in the winter of '77, Chrysalis began hard-selling Debbie in a manner that *Playboy* would find repugnant – running her picture beneath the invitation "Wouldn't You Like To Rip Her To Shreds?"

Chrysalis attracted the audience they considered fit for Debbie, and Debbie herself accommodated the chauvinistic Boy's Club toss-pots in a manner that would have made Xaviera Hollander seem militant. The sound was bad, Debbie was too busy being subservient to dance and the new material (later condemned to posterity on the "Plastic Letters" album) was dire. Debbie's philosophy on life? "My only concern is not to be old and dilapidated and not be able to make money."

In their bid for popularity, Blondie have since been reduced to digging up Fifties also-ran "Denise" as their one hit, *Sieg Heil*ing a West German audience ("Why shouldn't I?") and telling a journalist present at their sink-or-swim *Top Of The Pops* session – "Remember, we're Power Pop *not* Punk!"

Debbie Blondie is 34.

Like their dumb Blondie mentor, Snatch, Patti Smith and Cherry Vanilla all left it too late (their "life begins at" thirties) before pushing themselves as punky pin-ups.

Those who were not the power behind the throne (unlike Patti Smith, who has been supported since 1971 by her *Ménage-a-midget* with Allen Lanier of the Blue Oyster Cult and trendy Tom Verlaine) emigrated to lovable old London at the start of 1977 – where the scars on their arms would stand as proof of switch-blade scuffles instead of flesh confirmation that these girls sporting smell-of-smack failure black track-marks were nothing more than dealers' stooges.

Snatch were a duo comprised of Judy Nylon and Patti Palladin, the former's main claim to fame being that she once roomed with

Baldwin Eno, while the latter acts as an efficient connection for those sad souls forever waiting for their man. When the band split up after releasing two quasi-Heartbreakers smack-anthems, Judy faded back into New York while Patti used her credentials as a place-marker in Johnny Thunders' transitory band The Living Dead. Both would be more successful had they married baseball heroes.

Cherry Vanilla became one with RCA via a career as the arche-type alternative capitalist girl, performing in the Warhol freak-circus and – as chronicled in her "Pop Tart" biography – generally making a vocation out of being abused by numerous rock-star morons. If David Bowie's wife had not already made a merkin (a pubic wig, very popular in the USA) out of him with scandal-sheet revelations, then Cherry's previous employment as D.B.'s "publicist" was sure to unearth enough racy anecdotes to make her "Little Red Rooster" blush from the tip of his nose to the varnish on his toes.

Dave's label RCA promptly came up with not only a recording contract but also a massive promotion campaign for her album "Bad Girl" and her single "The Punk", both of which disappeared a day after they appeared.

Patti Smith started out as a poet backed by a solitary electric guitar in 1973 which in two years evolved into the band which signed to Arista and backed her on the best debut album of all time "Horses", following it up with a brace of decrepit ducks "Radio Ethiopia" and "Easter" plus Patti performing a party-piece of falling off-stage and breaking her neck. Despite her initial promise, the silly old biddy was last heard of writing for *Viva* (a kind of down-market *Cosmopolitan*).

Rock is a pedestal sport, as in being a monarch – whenever possible, a boy inherits the throne – females are not thought to be the stuff worship/idols are made for/of. Girls are expected to grovel in the mezzanine while the stud struts his stuff *up there*, while a girl with the audacity to go onstage is always jeered, sneered and leered up to – rock and roll is very missionary, very religious, very repressive.

A guitar in the hands of a man boasts COCK – the same instru-ment in female hands therefore (to a warped male mind) screams CASTRATION.

Thus Joan Jett and her band The Runaways are shrugged off as a novelty, and Joan herself tittered away as a teenage joke.

As a matter of fact, Joan is the only woman yet to eternally sub-jugate the heckling male audience down to its rightful station. Though pushed as idiot jail-bait (and her four fine albums since 1975 as the hot-wet outpourings of such), Joan Jett is the last rock and roll star – AS YOU KNOW IT – in the world.

Never again will glamour, youth, melody and desperation find their way onto a big-time stage within one teenage body. After Joan Jett, all Americans are peanuts.

Poly Styrene is the best thing about British punk rock while Joan Jett is the best thing about American punk rock. The difference between the two girls mirrors the gulf between the two countries.

Joan sees rock and roll as an end in itself, thinking to chant about hating parents, school and cops while loving sex, drugs and night-time is fulfilling the function of the music – to clumsily parody youth, rebellion and anger.

Poly, however, realises that without a genuine declaration of commitment and the exertion of whatever influence a musician may have, then rock and roll is pointless, useless, worthless.

# PEARLS AND SCUM

The establishment wants to maintain a controlled chaos which it dignifies as "law and order". If law and order were the real objectives of this country's ruling-class, provocative and pointless displays of aggression such as football matches and fascist marches – responsible for the constant waste of millions of police, pounds and property – would not be sacrosanct.

However, the working class must take their frustration out on someone, and who could possibly be a better target than more vulnerable members of their own social strata? So government approves football, political aggravation and – since the Fifties – the youth culture.

Capitalism – "the godfather of fascism" – lives to increase multi-million dollar profits. In "rock and roll", the particular interests of the establishment and capitalism fit together as compactly as a joint, finding an affinity that they are unable to achieve in any other business venture.

As soon as any ostensibly dangerous new musical phenomena appear in the sweaty clubs giving a righteous finger to the status quo, it is enticed in from the cold by the same old dangled carrots of sex/drugs/cash/fame and run through the mill of commercial assimilation. What were once sharp, angry fangs are rendered soft, ineffective gums.

By maintaining the music's illusion of youth rebellion it accomplishes its purpose – a green-back producer channelling not only the money but the time, energy and psyche of young people into what has been their most jealously guarded palliative for over twenty years.

Punk started as a movement born out of No Fun and ended as a product whose existence was No Threat.

The early Seventies (and all of the Sixties) were so 1920s, so ignorant in their innocence – until Eric Clapton, Rod Stewart and David Bowie shot off their drunken slobbering mouths in the middle year of the Seventies, who would have even *dreamed* that Rock could be anything *other* than Against Racism?

But as soon as that organisation fulfilled a need, and as soon as a white student and an Asian youth were murdered by racist sects, entertainment *à la* Gary Glitter and Bob Dylan – who in *their* time had every right to be apolitical – became a banal luxury.

It took the unrest that infested Britain after the white working-class had been turned on the non-white working-class to breed those trail-blazing, means-to-an-end messengers The Sex Pistols –

the first cannon-fodder to become stars. Their image and their energy shattered the glib facade – but their anger was too desultory, their vision too short-sighted, their aims too capricious for them to serve as anything more than a shock-troop vanguard for the few bands who dared to be against macho/dumbo music for rapists, against racism, against censorship and against all the grey forces.

Now, all rock/pop/soul/disco/punk/reggae/roll bands are either Pearls or Scum.

Next only to punk shot-by-both-sides political platitudes – "We hate fascists and we hate Commies too!", both before and after the Commies united with the blacks to win Lewisham! – the major omen of the genre's hoodwinking was its espousal of Reggae, Capital R For Rasta Full Stop. Not even *black* music which ever since it gave birth to rock and roll has discouraged racism and sexism in potentially reactionary kids through blues, Motown, Stax, Ska, Blue-Beat and disco.

Not even pre-punk reggae music, containing the admirable inherent morality of Desmond Dekker, Tapper Zukie and Steel Pulse – no, punk junked up any Rastafarian connection it could score, becoming so addicted to Rasta *in toto* that throughout 1977 and 1978 every "punk" show was preceded by interminable Rasta music.

Hatred of women is the foundation of fascism, but for sheer vitriolic venomous malignancy, the misogyny of the Rastafarians surpasses even that of Hitler's Nazis.

The archaic religion of the Rastas is lifted directly from the Old Testament, the Orthodox Jewish religion had not the modern Israelis realised that if their women were not equals (and not allowed to fight – the Rastas are too tiny and cranky a sect ever to be a threat) then their country would not survive.

Rastas consider a woman on her period to be "sick" and not fit to be in the presence of men. She is locked away, and on no account may she be permitted to contaminate the Rasta-man's food by cooking it for him. Rastas consider a woman's body must be covered at all times in long African dresses that touch the ground, and that she must never wear trousers which are the sole right of men. Rastas believe women who have abortions are using their bodies for "internal cemeteries".

To Rasta, man is Stud, woman a sperm receptacle, who couldn't possibly enjoy sex unless she was the lowest whore in Babylon. Rastas believe in God whom they call "Jah" and smoke dope all the time in the hope that this will help them communicate with him. Rastas believe that Haile Selassie (unsuccessful military dictator of Ethiopia, ousted by invading Italians in 1936) is the Son of God.

Rastas preach black supremacy, and prophesy that unless they return to Africa by 1983 the world must perish.

Had this view since been refuted by contemporary idols Dillinger, Black Slate and batty bald-head Bob Marley, then their rights would be worth standing up for. As it is, who would raise a hand if the National Front treated the Rastas as the Rastas treat their women?

"I'm more opposed to the National Abortion Campaign than I am to the National Front", boasts Black Slate bassist Elroy. He emphasises with a smile – "You get certain African tribes where the woman, if she's seen gets stoned. Stoned."

So if Jah's so omnipotent, how come the only act to get a black ethnic Seventies number one record are GIRLS? Althia and Donna, who scored the dual victory of kicking both the National Front youth-recruitment scheme *and* the Rasta *Sieg Heil*, male masterplan in their silicone-overgrown balls.

Top of the charts in early 1978, Althia and Donna's "Uptown Top Ranking" was the kind of reggae that Marley and the rest were too serious, too stoned and too stupid to make; infectiously contagious dance music, with the girls playfully though determinedly deriding the disapproving gazes of the Rastamen as they make their gleeful way to the Top Rank dance-hall up-town, dressed in their halter-backs and high-heels – Althia and Donna, that is, not the Rasta-men!!!

Strictly Seventies is Rastafarianism ... but such an all-boys-together aura hangs over punk – those one-sex pogo-packs down The Roxy, that lack of new wave love songs – that one wonders if it's anything more than the lolling-in-the-mud New a.k.a. No Morality of the Sixties; sharing your girl just to get to your best buddy.

These days, rock music challenges football as a refuge for those manly (arse) souls who do not think finding no love in a thousand girls and doing alright with the boys is a cause for concern.

The private armies who devotedly follow bands around the country – The Lewisham Boys begat by Sham 69, The Poplar Boys begat by Cock Sparrer, The Stranglers' Finchley Boys (who have ended up running errands for their band's label) – do they just dislike girls?

OR ARE THEY JUST CLOSET CASES?

The back-to-grass-roots philosophy promoted by the emergence of punk in mid-1976 spawned an "alternative" press in the guise of the fanzine epidemic, and also a healthy "alternative" to the stranglehold of the major recording corporations in the form of the independent record labels.

But by mid-1977 both the fanzine press and the small labels had degenerated from what was initially a potentially worthwhile project into an over-priced, green-eyed, pale imitation of all they had purported to detest.

Started by working-class kids at the end of 1976, fanzining soon became a fashionable public-school sport. By mid '77 the fanzines were wallowing in the mire of a golden age long gone; duplicated, sated drivel written by obnoxious whiners for over-grown wimps. Half-full of tin-pot tirades against the thriving orthodox rock papers, half-full of the golden calves of punk – collages of the Queen, the Pistols and second-hand newspaper headlines blaring unemployment and anarchy but meant to imply Armageddon – they were nothing for something at an average price of 25p. You would have done better putting your pennies towards a picture-sleeved single.

And that Deptford doyenne of fanzines himself, Mark Perry of *Sniffin' Glue* (what a girl), became just another Blast Furnace when he shut up his printing press after *Sniffin' Glue*'s twelfth issue. In this farewell edition he enclosed the free gift (no one would buy it!) of his newly-formed band's first single – thus perpetuating the limp myth that all music journalists are frustrated front-men.

Perry sold his Airfix-eroded integrity for £500 by flogging the rights of the *Sniffin' Glue Brittanica* to the ancient manager of Gaye's Adverts, who published them as a £2 paperback, *The Best of Sniffin' Glue.* It thereby joined the ranks of the long line of ex-punk-ploitation books, all written under sweat-shop, slave-labour conditions by the wretched Fan-Scenes.

Mark Perry was last seen with Wayne County on his knee.

Similarly, the independent record labels were usually founded on a loan of about £400 (the amount that Berry Gordy started his Tamla Motown empire with in the first month of 1959) and run on a shoe-string budget from one minute office.

Whereas the major labels haphazardly flung enormous quantities of vinyl at the weekly charts, in the hope that somehow, somewhere, something had to stick, and were used to a single either dying a fast death with sales of a few hundred or else becoming a hit record selling upwards of 25,000 copies, the small labels pressed 2000 records for £300 by bands considered too left-field, too off-beat, too much of a minority taste to sign with a major, and at first sold every copy and still had change from the £300 to pay royalties.

At first, the musicians recording with the independents were genuine talents who – even if not strictly punk – could find an audience in the least-blinkered new wave market. But the proof just wasn't in the product, and soon every bunch of no-hopers in the Western world shoved out their aural refuse on their own indulgent label, while the best of the independent's bands were snapped up by a major (who always used the gullible, ego-inflated independents as an "alternative" *New Faces*).

Where the record shops who did not deal only in the Top Fifty had once been dizzily prepared to take a dozen copies of a small label's latest release, by mid-1977 the standard of product had declined to such an all-time low that they had to have their arms twisted to take even one independent 45 – and then only on a strict sale-or-return basis.

By following exactly the same policy of no quality control as the enormous corporations, the small independents killed it for themselves.

Started in July 1976 by ex-roadies Andrew Jakeman-Riviera and Dave Robinson, Stiff Records was an independent label which acted as a convalescent home for old hippies (haircut optional) such as Devo, Pink Fairies, The Damned, Larry Wallis, Motorhead and The Tony Tyla Gang – all of them ripe for a ride on the "new wave" band-wagon and thus helping it become a write-off.

All in all, Stiff was a label erected on the momentum of the resentment – "I'll show them!" – that chases inadequacy. And fittingly, the careers of Stiff's triplet stars – Ian Dury, Elvis Costello and Nick Lowe – were built upon a similar ever-shortness.

Nick Lowe is a middle-aged, multi-chinned senile cynic with a split ends basin-cut and sweaty armpits, who has based his entire career on plagiarising the ideas of others. His solitary Stiff single was lifted from Chuck Berry, and when he left the label (along with Elvis Costello) in 1977 to join ex-Chilli Willi manager's company Radar, he cut an album which truly earned him his title – "The Dork Of Derivative". In this, Lowe blatantly ripped-off and watered-down Jonathan Richman, David Bowie, The Jackson Five, Chuck Berry (again), The Beatles, Kenneth Anger, 10cc, The Beach Boys and Tommy Rowe.

"I'm just a hack tunesmith", grovels Nicholas. "I don't think of myself as a song-writer. I just *steal* the stuff. I want to be rich, I want to sell. 90 per cent of the world are fools."

Nick Lowe's musical handicap is that he is not one of the lucky 10 per cent. Ian Dury and Elvis Costello were pub-rockers seeking a second bite at the banana by pushing a contrived, calculated image – Dury the waggish barrow-chappie (who didn't spend nearly a decade in art schools, honestly) and Costello the resentful, impotent myopic who appeared out of nowhere and promptly took over the scene (and didn't spend years slogging away at pubs and folk-clubs, cross our hearts).

Both cut one toe-tapping album each, on which their whining was disguised by catchy couplets; but they spoiled as they dallied too long slobbering over their insignificant ego deficiencies until, as Tallulah Bankhead said, there was "less there than meets the eye".

Remember – if it's on Stiff or Radar, it ain't worth a fart.

The chart-rigging scandal of early 1978, in which it was revealed that dreck vinyl could be bought into the Bottom Twenty of the Top Fifty, totally overlooked the fact that payola is a way of life in the music business, taking place before the record gets onto the market. The payola is subtle and legal – DJs and journalists get free lunches, free tickets, free trips to America and a staple diet of free albums, which are stored in the press office of the record company.

Two years ago, a loser *Sounds* writer who was also a junkie supported his habit by a daily tour of the labels for boxes of product, which he would immediately sell to a West End record shop which makes a large part of its profit from buying unplayed albums half-price from the spoilt brats of the rock press.

However, some music business hype (short for "hyperbole") is as subtle as a hippo turd. In autumn 1977, mouth almighties Sham 69 played on the roof of the 24-hour Vortex Coffee Bar (associated with the Vortex Club, the Vortex album, the Vortex fanzine and the Vortex Record Shoppe) in an effort to promote its opening.

When police were called to quell the disturbance, lead singer James Sham demanded of onlookers, "Are we disturbing you, me old cock sparrers?" They were speechless, so James decided "Stone me, it's the voice of the people!" and carried on with his cavortings.

The carefully-assembled punks and journalists were thereupon treated to a public arrest as James was marched off to Tottenham Court Road police station on a charge of "threatening behaviour", and later released on £500 bail (not in public).

Later that day, the Vortex Record Shoppe received their first shipment of a thousand copies of Sham 69's first single "I Don't Wanna". The record was flogged in a sleeve touting a picture of an anti-Nazi Lewisham demonstrator being violently arrested by police, and was intended to succour the punter into believing that this was the martyred James Sham being peacefully nicked on the roof of the Vortex. The single was pitifully promoted with record company badges bearing the legend "James Is Innocent".

It flopped – miserably.

But by this time, every old tart in the world who wore a £200 Zandra Rhodes "conceptual punk chic" dress complete with rips, zips and safety pins, had read the punk beauty hints in *19* and was scoffing their scampi off a table littered with punk-leather napkin-holders (as featured in *Vogue*). The Punk's New Clothes enabled the raddled old hags of sub-*Debrett* debris to put off their much-needed face-lift for just one more year. Flower-power music papers like *Sounds*; hairdressers like *Schumi*; old actresses like Jenny Runacre; old hacks like Lester Bangs; old groupies like Marianne Faithfull; old fashion magazines like *Ritz*; old DJs like John Peel; old film directors like Derek Jarman; old haberdashers like Malcolm McLaren . . . all would have done well to heed the advice that James Maxton gave on the occasion of Ramsay MacDonald's last speech:

"SIT DOWN, MAN. YOU'RE A BLOODY TRAGEDY."

Hopefully, by this time next year the entire cast-list of *Berk's Peerage* plus above-listed bum-wipes will have caught onto what at the start of 1978 failed to out-fad punk as the latest big bad craze – Power Pop.

Led by The Rutles and The Mop Turds, Power Pop bands wear fringes and suits and bounce around the stage looking wholesome and fat. They pretend that they love their audience, and that their "movement" is something more than an itchy-fingered entrepreneur's off-moment. When legless on half a shandy, they can be heard yelling that they are bigger than God.

The out-of-time punker anachronisms deride the Power Sloppers for their superficiality, though both punky-wavers and poppers have proved equally insipid, innocuous and ineffectual when it comes to being any more of a threat to the norm than the Girl Guides. Both the clueless coteries should follow the example of the 14 obscure Californian punk combos who played two sell-out seven-hour shows in San Francisco – raising $4,000 for the striking miners of Stearns County, Kentucky.

And while the perennial Rock Rebels blather on about "commitment" and "fighting the good fight", it is left to the international showbusiness set to put principles before profits in playing benefits for Erin Pizzey's battered wives – Cleo Laine and Lynsey De Paul – and protesting against the vicious mass-slaughter of dolphins by the Japanese – Olivia Newton-John and Helen Reddy – by forsaking fortunes when they cancelled their tours of the country.

Paradoxically, the finest thing to come out of punk (at least, to come out of the space cleared by punk) was the finest thing to come out of music. The Tom Robinson Band were formed in January 1977 as a direct result of the growing right-wing rock element, after Tom Robinson realised that he could never fight facism, racism and sexism (or be a commercial success) playing acoustic guitar in a closet.

The Tom Robinson Band are Tom Robinson (vocals and bass), Danny Kustow (guitar), Nick Plytas (keyboards) and Dolphin Taylor (drums), and in the autumn of 1977 they became EMI's first noticeable signing since The Sex Pistols.

Their first single "Motorway" was the spoonful of sugar needed to persuade EMI to give the band total artistic control, as it sped up the charts backed by *Top Of The Pops* appearances in the winter of '77. Buyers of the record may have taken the clenched fist on the front of the sleeve as nothing more than the band's personalised punky pose motif – but there was no mistaking the message of the B-side and the reverse sleeve. A picture of convicted armed-robber George Ince, a version of Bob Dylan's "I Shall Be Released" and the telephone number of the "Free George Ince Campaign".

The hit-buying public were still wondering what this clean-cut kid on the box could possibly have to do with a convicted criminal when the quadro-A-sided "Rising Free" EP was released to give them the answer. Whatever their preconceptions about feminism ("Right On Sister"), beating up police ("Martin"), anti-capitalism ("Don't Take No For An Answer") and homosexuality ("Sing If You're Glad To Be Gay"), the "masses" seem to be more reasonable than they're given credit for, because "Rising Free" became the band's second consecutive hit at the start of 1978. This time, the reverse sleeve bore the Tom Robinson Band's fan club address and the telephone number of the Gay Switchboard.

When not recording their call-to-arms Smash-the-Front album material – "Up Against The Wall", "Ain't Gonna Take It No More", "Winter of '79", "Power In The Darkness", "Long Hot Summer" and "Better Decide Which Side You're On" – the Tom Robinson Band play benefits for battered wives, against homosexual persecution and for the Anti-Nazi League.

They are the first band not to shrug off their political stance as soon as they walk out of the recording studio. The first band with sufficient pure, undiluted unrepentant bottle to keep their crooning necks firmly on the uncompromising line of commitment when life would be infinitely easier – and no less of a commercial success – if they made their excuses and left before the riot.

Compared to the Tom Robinson Band, every other rock musician is wanking into the wind.

**ASHES**

You, kid! Come here. . . .

You wanna "Capital Radio" EP? You wanna black bag EMI "Anarchy"? You wanna A&M "God Save The Queen"? You wanna French 12-inch "Anarchy"? You wanna "Anarchy In The USA" bootleg? You wanna collect butterflies?

Very fulfilling, collecting things ... very satisfying. Keep you satisfied, make you sated, make you fat and old and cold, queueing for the rock and roll show.

In 1978 every record company is waking up to find a somewhat superfluous punk combo on its doorstep. Supply and demand? But you can't supply something that there's no demand for.

Never mind, kid, there'll soon be another washing-machine/spot-cream/rock-band on the market to solve all your problems and keep you quiet/off the street/distracted from the real enemy/content till the next pay-day.

Anyhow, God Save Rock And Roll ... it made you a Consumer, a potential Moron. . . .

IT'S ONLY ROCK AND ROLL AND IT'S PLASTIC, PLASTIC, YES IT IS!!!!!!